Food for the Soul

Food for the Soul

Selections from the
Holy Apostles Soup Kitchen
Writers' Workshop

Elizabeth Maxwell and **Susan Shapiro**, Editors

Introduction by **Ian Frazier**

Seabury Books
An imprint of Church Publishing, New York

The Writers' Workshop is made possible with public funds from the New York State Council on the Arts, a State Agency.

A catalog record for this book is available from the Library of Congress

ISBN 01-59627-001-2

Church Publishing Incorporated
445 Fifth Avenue
New York, NY 10016
www.churchpublishing.org

5 4 3 2 1

To all members of the Holy Apostles
Writers' Workshop past and present
and in memory of
Clarence A. Clarke, Pierce McLoughlin, & Janice English

List of Contributors

Bill Acheson, Nelson Blackman, Damita Boston, John Cabello, Clarence A. Clarke, Norman Clayton, Paul Coleman, Ronnie Eisen, Janice English, Thyatira English, George Glass, Dorothy Jackson, Donald Mackey, Pierce McLoughlin, Joe Negrelli, Peter Nkruma, Leucio Parella, Jeff Rubin, Walter Schubert, Muhammad Siagha, Ted Sikorski, Jay Stockman, Tory Connolly Walker, Carol West, and Mitch Wiater

Acknowledgments

One of the joys of this project has been getting to know an incredible number of generous and gifted people who have helped in one way or another. Our deepest gratitude goes to:

Matthew Flamm, Brian McDonald, Stan Mieses, Kate Reed, and Alec Wilkinson, all of whom taught in the program with great dedication;

Our typists: Sam Soffer, Jenny Traslavina, Kate Reed, and Claudia Haygooni, who patiently deciphered hand-written manuscripts and produced an anthology of each year of the workshop, and Devan Sipher, whose skill with computers and copy editing made the preparation of this manuscript infinitely easier;

Nelson Blackman, for his fabulous photographs;

Carol West, for her perseverance and creativity in tracking down missing writers;

the Reverend Bill Greenlaw, for his leadership in fostering radical hospitality at Holy Apostles, and his support of the Writers' Workshop;

the Holy Apostles staff who have been vitally involved in making the workshop happen over the years: John Ruiz, Clyde Kuemmerle, Stacy Alan, Neville Hughes, Evelyn Israel, Janet Gracey, Jacqueline Feyjoo, Wendy Shepherd, Linda Adams, and the soup kitchen crew;

the Lila Wallace Reader's Digest Fund, which gave the money and impetus to start the workshop, and the New York State Council on the Arts, which has generously granted funds to keep it going;

the warm and wonderful staff at Seabury Books, including Ken Arnold, Joan Castagnone, Patti Byrns, and Parul Sardana, as well as the writer/literary matchmaker Connie Kirk and the agent Elizabeth Kaplan, who generously donated her time and expertise.

Most of all, we thank the writers for sharing their stories with such courage, grace, and heart. They are the ones who make the workshop happen, and who make it all worthwhile.

Table of Contents

Foreword

Sometimes people ask me why we have a writing workshop in a soup kitchen. "Isn't this frivolous?" they say. "Shouldn't you be focusing on the basic human needs: food, clothing, shelter?" Over the years, I have come to respond that writing—telling one's story—is a basic human need. Writing is food for the soul.

Food and the soul are both important at Holy Apostles. Holy Apostles Soup Kitchen, the major outreach project of the Church of the Holy Apostles, is the largest emergency feeding program in New York City, and in the Episcopal Church nationally. Our mission is to end hunger, and in the meantime, to feed all those who come to us during the hours we are open, no questions asked. These days, that means we feed between eleven hundred and thirteen hundred people every Monday through Friday, holidays included. Knowing that those who eat here spend much of their time trying to justify their existence to one bureaucracy or another, we try to welcome them as our honored guests: to receive them as Christ, as the scripture enjoins. Some days we do this better than others, and it's easier with some guests than others. But having the intention makes a difference. It helps us see the whole person and not just homelessness, or mental illness, or addiction, or even horrible bad luck.

Monday through Friday between 10:30 a.m. and 12:30 p.m., we serve a hot meal to the hungry men and women who line up outside our door. We know that this is the only meal of the day for some of them, so we aim for high calories and as complete nutrition as we can manage. A typical menu might include spaghetti and meat sauce, peas and carrots, cabbage salad, sliced peaches, bread, and iced tea. Word on the street rates us a four-star soup kitchen. Some people go through several times. We figure that means they need to.

The crowd eating at Holy Apostles is a pretty diverse representation of humanity. There are blacks, whites, Latinos, native New Yorkers, and immigrants from Africa, Eastern Europe, and Central America. There are mostly men but some women and children, an age range from infancy to eighty or older, Christians, Jews, Muslims, and atheists; bike messengers, transvestites, and college graduates; some who have been on the street for years and others who never thought they would eat in a soup kitchen. Our volunteers are as varied as our guests. Welcoming that diversity has had an impact on the parish that is palpable. We have learned to be open to people and ideas that seemed inconceivable before. It stretches us and our faith.

At Holy Apostles, we know that soup kitchens are not the answer to the problem of hunger. We are involved in education and political advocacy to try to change the systems that allow hunger and homelessness to exist in the richest country in the world. Through our counseling and referrals program, we also work with people individually to try to help them find their way out of poverty and off the soup kitchen line. Housed in a construction trailer in the church's driveway, our counselors help people find shelter, a warm coat, a job, a detox program—and some hope that they matter and things can get better. We also host a legal clinic, a medical van, representatives of the Veteran's Administration, HIV outreach workers, and even volunteer chiropractors, all of whom offer help that our guests need.

Holy Apostles Soup Kitchen began during the recession of the early 1980s. Hungry people were hanging out in a park across the street from the church, and some of them came to our door asking for food. Holy Apostles' rector at the time, the Reverend Rand Frew, went to the vestry and proposed that he raise the money to open a soup kitchen—an emergency program that would help tide our neighbors over in hard times that would surely be very temporary. The vestry gave the go-ahead, Father Rand (somewhat to their amazement) raised $50,000, the doors opened on October 22, 1982, and on that first day thirty-five people were fed.

From those modest beginnings, the soup kitchen has grown exponentially. Along the way, we have discovered that people all around New York and beyond care about what we are doing and are willing to support us, both financially and through volunteering. We really could not exist without the tremendous energy and commitment of our volunteers—some forty-five every day who come from every walk of life to serve the food, clean the tables, welcome our guests, and staff the counseling and referrals program. At the same time, the soup kitchen staff has grown from two in 1982—a chef and a project director—to eighteen full-time and eight part-time employees today, some of them former guests. We served 287,275 meals in 2003, with a budget of $2.2 million. We raise that money with a lot of sweat and prayer, from generous individuals, foundations, and corporate donors. Government provides less than 20 percent, and religious organizations only about 5 percent. Sometimes we wonder where the money will come from, or if it will. So far, we are amazed by grace on a regular basis.

On April 9, 1990, the Church of the Holy Apostles suffered a devastating fire. The next day, the soup kitchen served a cold meal by candlelight. Standing in line with the smell of smoke still in the air, a guest offered me a few dollars from his pockets to help fix the church. As we began to rebuild, the parish realized that we had the opportunity to design a space that embraced a constituency beyond our own congregation. The restored church, a flexible-use space with no pews, is also the main dining room of the Holy Apostles Soup Kitchen. The building has been designated a landmark by the City of New York Landmarks Preservation Commission, proving that the preservation of historic beauty need not conflict with meeting present need. Our guests eat their meals at round tables in the nave under soaring arches. Light comes in the historic windows—Holy Apostles' greatest architectural treasure—in jewel tones. The diners seem to feel comfortable here, to know it as their place too. I believe the beauty of the space adds something to the meal, whether those eating are consciously aware of it or not.

Father Bill Greenlaw, Holy Apostles' rector and the executive director of the Soup Kitchen, likes to say that the meal we serve during the week stems directly from the meal we share on Sunday morning. In that meal we believe that we are fed with the very love and life of God, a love that is breathtaking in its boldness and vulnerability, its willingness to embrace every part of our human condition. As we gather at the table we remember Jesus, who spent much of his time eating and drinking with friends who included the outcasts of his day. We recall sacred stories of hospitality, loaves and fishes, a mysterious stranger recognized when bread is blessed and broken. In church, we share food, and we tell stories.

This brings me, at last, to the Writers' Workshop. I am a preacher, and sometimes I cannot keep myself from theology. Most of the stories that are told by the participants are not explicitly religious, but they are sacred stories nonetheless. They are about deep stuff, light stuff, soul stuff. They are hilarious, tragic, raw, flippant, magical. They are poetry, prose, rap, memoir. For me, they are especially poignant because they speak both to the unique experiences of homeless people coming to a soup kitchen and to the joys and sorrows that are common to us all.

Perhaps I love this program so much because it is surprising. When Ian Frazier came to me ten years ago with the idea for a writing workshop for the soup kitchen guests, I was not sure that people would stay around after the meal for something so intangible. I was quickly and happily surprised by the dedication and commitment of the writers to the program. In the years since, I have continued to be surprised and deeply moved by the passion the participants have for the workshop, and by the stories they are brave enough to tell. I have also been touched by the generosity, commitment, and skill of the teachers. In my experience, there is something mysterious about writing anyway, and it seems that this is so also for our workshop participants. The words come from a new place inside them, and they discover things about themselves as they write. They realize what happened, they find out something unexpected about who they are, they access their creativity and their talent.

Over the years, Ian and his co-teachers have created a wonderfully safe space in which a real community of writers can flourish, and that too is a surprise and a blessing: support for the storytelling and the development of a craft. The public readings have been an astonishing culmination of each year's workshop, as the participants share their writing with a larger community. Some have been published in newspapers and magazines as well, to their amazed delight. Now this work goes out into the world, and I hope that it will help its readers see many things—from homeless people to human possibilities, from shoes to first love to New York City—with new eyes.

Writing—telling a story with heart and courage and the best skill a writer can muster—nourishes the one who tells it. It changes you, somehow. It is indeed food for the soul. Hearing such stories is soul food too. I trust that you who read them will also be nourished by this remarkable work.

ELIZABETH MAXWELL
Associate Rector, The Church of the Holy Apostles

Introduction

The Making of the Holy Apostles Writers' Workshop

BY IAN FRAZIER

When the Lila Wallace Reader's Digest Fund offered me a grant back in 1993 to set up an arts program with the nonprofit community organization of my choice, I thought immediately of the Church of the Holy Apostles Soup Kitchen. It's the largest soup kitchen in the city, and one of the largest in the country. All churches talk about Christ's teachings—here was a church that took his injunction about feeding the hungry and put it into practice on a big-city scale, lovingly and effectively, every working day. I admired this enormously, and in the years in which I've come to know the church better my admiration has only increased.

The original idea, as I explained it to the church's clergy, William Greenlaw and Elizabeth Maxwell, was to invite soup kitchen guests to come to a workshop every Wednesday after lunch and write essentially whatever they felt like for forty minutes. Then we—instructors and participants—would spend another forty minutes reading our work aloud and commenting. Each week a typist would type up the handwritten manuscripts and photocopy them. The writers could then make corrections and additions as they chose. After nine or a dozen sessions we would take the work and collect it in spiral-bound books—copied and bound at Kinko's—for the church and the writers to have, and we would also hold a free public reading at the church by all the writers who wanted to read their work for an audience. The

Reverends Greenlaw and Maxwell kindly agreed to the plan, and in this fairly simple and straightforward way the workshop has proceeded ever since.

To see how many soup kitchen guests would be interested in writing, I sat by the soup kitchen exit one lunchtime and talked to anyone who had a minute before they left. Dozens of people stopped to talk. Almost everybody who did told me they knew a story they would like to write. At the end of lunch I had a list of over fifty people who said they would come to the first session.

In fact, that many participants did not show up. The other instructors and I would learn that the demands of living on the street make writing—no easy pursuit in the first place—a sometimes un-meetable challenge for many soup kitchen guests. In our first year, however, we soon had a lively and talented core group of about 9 who came regularly to the sessions. Remarkable pieces of writing began to emerge at every class. To give inspiration a path, the instructors (Bob Blaisdell and I, the first year) would suggest a couple of topics, to be used or ignored as the participants chose. "Shoes," "My Best Mistake," "Ten Rules for Living," and "A Wild Ride" are topics I remember from that year.

By now we've had more than 250 participants in the program. Jay Stockman, Donald Mackey, Carol West, Mitch Wiater, and John Cabello, all of whom took part in our tenth year, have been with the workshop since the beginning (or almost). The writers who attend regularly form a warm and encouraging group every year, and when the sessions come to an end we're sorry to lose that Wednesday camaraderie. Yet the workshop owes a lot, too, to participants who have attended only once or twice. Many of those remain in the front of my mind when I think back over the workshop. At one of the first sessions a man came who had gone through (as many participants have) drug and alcohol problems. Now he was in a twelve-step program. He sat down and wrote a wild, headlong, intergalactic science-fiction-like saga of a battle between beings named Good, Evil, Addiction, and the

Higher Power. The man was from the Deep South, and as he read the story in his Mississippi Delta accent we were bowled over. I never saw him again, but I hope he got a fraction as much from his one time at the workshop as we got from hearing the piece he wrote.

At the beginning of the program I underestimated or just didn't grasp the size of the sufferings many workshop participants had in their lives. I don't want to make light of these hardships now when I say that a main feature of the Writers' Workshop has been that it is fun. It's fun to write something cool and funny and heartfelt and effortless-seeming and then read it to friendly listeners who get a kick out of it. It's satisfying, too (if not exactly fun), to write a self-revealing cry or shout and lay it out for people to see, and to find patterns and beauty even in pain. Writing can be a kind of trampoline that bounces you higher until you glimpse the possibility of never coming down. It's one of the noble acts humans do, and almost always it ennobles those who do it.

In New York City, and in America, people of all sorts and conditions and backgrounds get together to create works greater and finer than they could achieve alone. You see it on the street every day. At the West Fourth Street playground in Greenwich Village guys play pick-up basketball games that reach levels of skill indistinguishable from the pros; on 42nd Street hat-passing musicians are blowing harmonicas that lift pedestrians right off their feet; on a stalled F train, a lady makes a funny remark that earns a laugh from the whole car and gets us all talking about our predicament. We collaborate, and what you can do—how well you play, how compellingly you write— is more important than you are. Gifts are distributed generously and widely, by God's grace. It's a pleasure, and it's an honor, to read these pieces by gifted participants of the Writers' Workshop at the Church of the Holy Apostles.

Reflections

Learning from My Students

BY SUSAN SHAPIRO

It was ten o'clock on a cold Wednesday morning in March 1996 at the Church of the Holy Apostles in Chelsea. More than a thousand people were already waiting in line around the block for the free lunch. Wearing my old jeans and sweatshirt, I didn't look out of place. Somebody complained that I was cutting in line. I searched for my fellow teachers, Bob Blaisdell and Ian Frazier, who had started the grassroots-writing group with a grant the spring before. I found them both at a table on the sidelines of the dining room under a "Writers' Workshop" sign, next to tables for TB testing and petitions against welfare reform.

After they finished eating, many soup kitchen regulars stopped by to talk to us. They asked questions about the program and wanted to enroll. Since a few gave no last names or addresses, Bob marked down descriptions. A big unshaven white man named Tim said he would come. I looked over Bob's shoulder. Bob wrote down, "Tall scary guy." A man with a Spanish accent named Juan said, "Been there, done that." When we asked what he meant, he said he had been in a prison-writing group in 1975 with John Cheever. "He got the Pulitzer Prize for his book *Falconer*, what did I get?" Juan asked, walking away. Seventy-four signed up for the workshop. Ten showed.

At 1 p.m. in a small room in a corner of the church, we commenced. Sitting on beige fold-out chairs around an oblong table, we gave out free notebooks and pens and introduced ourselves. Clarence, an older black man with glasses and white mustache, said he was from Jamaica, where he had worked for the government. Wanda, a hyper thirtyish woman in a smock dress, said she was "younger than a rainbow, older than a smile," then switched to French. In broken English, forty-one-year-old Mitch, who had dark hair and a mustache, spoke of missing his wife and son in Poland, and asked why we were doing this. I'm not sure we knew exactly why. Ian said, "Writing is a way of organizing experience and defying loss." Bob said you don't write to gain money or fame, but because you have an important story that must be told. I said that for me, writing was a way of turning the worst things in life into something funny or poignant or beautiful.

Twelve people, from ages eighteen to eighty, showed up fairly regularly for the next eleven Wednesday afternoons. Each week the teachers suggested two topics, which included "How I Came to New York," "If I Hadn't Seen It, I Wouldn't Have Believed It," "When One Door Closes, Another Opens," "My First Love," "So I Lied," and "My Best Mistake." The writers in the workshop scrawled furiously. Then, one at a time, they read their work aloud. When they finished reading, fellow scribes clapped, or nodded, or made such comments as, "You tell 'em, baby," or "Amen, ain't that the truth?"

Wanda's first piece began, "Abandoned by eight families: foster, step, and blood." L.M.S., a twenty-five-year-old wearing a baseball cap, wrote, "Where is my home, my true home, my twin home, my self-employed home?" Harriet, a pale woman in her fifties with long silver hair, revealed in a story that she had been raped at gunpoint in Brooklyn ten years before. I told Harriet I thought her piece was very brave and she hugged me. Wanda gave me a bottle of soda and thanked me for "my good energy." Clarence shared his cryptic prose about religion. His work wasn't personal. In fact it was almost anti-confessional, which seemed at odds with his warm, open demeanor.

Each Wednesday, Clarence came a half hour early and we would drink tea and catch up, as if we were old family friends. We were an odd couple. He was sixty-eight and Jamaican, a former government clerk in a beige three-piece suit, explaining Christian Science to a thirty-five-year-old Jewish poet in black Levi's and black tee-shirt who lived in Greenwich Village. I showed him a poem I wrote about getting my heart broken on the beautiful white sands of Negril, which he said was "very moving."

The first year I co-taught the workshop I was going through a rough time. Trying to quit my long-term two-pack-a-day cigarette habit, I was feeling nervous and depressed. Clarence had quit smoking twenty years earlier "with the faith of Jesus," so he gave me practical tips (drink a lot of tea, water, and chew on straws) and pep talks. Everyone wrote long, autobiographical, gritty stories about their own experiences. Clarence penned a few paragraphs about lost souls, heaven, and the acceptance of a higher power. Was it from the Bible? A.A.?

The next session, Alan, a funny, middle-aged former thespian with a cane, wrote, "From the moment Gary and I met with his famous opening words, 'I know what you want,' until his death 20 years later from lymphoma cancer, there wasn't anything we wouldn't do for each other." Walter, seventy-three, with gray hair and beard, chronicled how his father had become a penniless alcoholic in Bonny Old Scotland decades before. L.M.S. told Harriet to stop chomping on potato chips, because he couldn't concentrate. She put them away, then whispered, "But it helps me remember." T.C., five-foot-five and from Connecticut, wrote about receiving second- and third-degree burns on his face and having to wear a Jobst garment for six weeks. It looked like a silk stocking and T.C. was afraid the bank guard would think he was a robber. So he called the bank first to explain, because "I didn't want him panicking and shooting me." Clarence kept writing abstractions about sin and salvation.

As in the writing classes I had taught at New York University and the New School, the participants were curious about agents, book deals, and screenplays. Although Ian didn't want to use up workshop time for that, I gave out my business card to anyone who asked.

Clarence called first, just to say that he would be late the next week. Harriet called next, asking if she could show me essays by a friend of hers at the shelter. They both apologized for bothering me at home, but I was pleased they were starting to trust me. Trust did not come easy for the writing workshop members. Some were homeless, hurt, unemployed, poor, and in trouble. They had been kicked around a lot and were cynical, understandably apprehensive about opening up to a stranger, even a well-meaning, bleeding-heart liberal.

On the tenth week, Clarence wrote his first poem that I could easily understand, with colloquial language and natural imagery. This one was about the "wandering cedar" with "gnarled, crackly, and slender branches." It ended: "Little birds reach the blossoms/vying with the bees whose work lies among pollen and nectar./The wise patient old owl/rests on one leg, one owlish eye peering, the other closed." I analyzed it endlessly, trying to figure it out like a secret code. Was it about hope? Was he the wise old owl or the wandering cedar?

I counted eleven members at the final reading we gave at the church, the last Wednesday night in May. After short speeches by Ian and the Reverend Elizabeth Maxwell, T.C. read "My Face." Mitch read "Ten Rules for Living," which ended "Try to be happy even when you are not happy." Walter wanted to read his entire opus on Scotland, but Bob told him that ten pages were all we had time for. I kept turning toward the door, disappointed that Clarence didn't show. But he ran in late, apologizing, just in time to read two poems. There was a little party later, with food and soda, and I took group pictures. Several asked about the nonfiction adult education courses I was teaching. I wrote down the time, day, and address of my university class and told them to stop by anytime.

The next week, in my lecture hall, I found Clarence, Harriet, and Alan, who said, "I just schlepped forty blocks with my cane in the rain, so this better be good." Clarence came up to me afterwards to say that he would be sending me new work soon. When I told him I had submitted the group's work to a literary journal, he seemed pleased. A letter and poem from Clarence arrived in the mail a few days later. On lined notebook paper in blue pen, the letter said, "Lately I have detected the revival of something dear. I am inspired. Please be prepared for more of my poetry. Thank you so much. I love you."

Although I had only known Clarence a short time, I loved him too, like a favorite student, or maybe like the daughter or granddaughter he didn't have. There was no return address on the envelope and he had never given me his phone number. (Did he have one?) I hoped he would write, phone, or come sit in my class again. But a week later, someone from the Bellevue morgue called to say that Clarence had died of a heart attack. My business card was the only card in his wallet. Was I next of kin?

In the picture from that May reading, Clarence is standing in the front row, wearing a blue jacket, gray pants, and a red tie, proudly holding up the yellow book of everyone's writing (which Bob and Ian prepared for the members as a keepsake). The poetry editor called to say that she was printing some of the work I had sent her, including a poem by Clarence, and that she would send me copies, but the journal never came.

After that spring, I looked at people on the streets of New York differently, to see if I recognized them. Once I thought I saw Clarence on the subway, but the elderly man in his coat turned out to be someone else. I kept his last poem in my purse and reread it many times, remembering what he, and the writing group, taught me: "A hundred moans/songs like rising thrones/seeking redemption."

Ten Years Later

BY BOB BLAISDELL

We have completed ten years of the Holy Apostles Soup Kitchen Writers' Workshop. There need be no end. Over those ten years, more than two hundred and fifty people have participated in writing about their lives and visions.

Every early spring, Wednesday afternoons have been a joyful time for me and the church a joyful place. For its freedom and camaraderie, the Writers' Workshop has been like no other writing class or group I have known. As an instructor it has been as challenging as it is rewarding. When I joined Ian Frazier on his adventure that first year, 1995, we had no idea what would or could happen. "Why write?" some of the soup kitchen patrons would ask us as we advertised our class from an exit-way table. Why, indeed? We assured them it was worth a try.

After lunch service concluded, we would meet the participants at a table in an alcove of the church or out in a trailer office. We all would talk a little about life and a little about writing, and then we, the instructors, would suggest topics based on sayings, proverbs, idiomatic expressions, song titles, and peculiar autobiographical themes. We all would write for forty minutes and then read around, listening to each other's words, with participants and instructors both making helpful or curious remarks about the stories, essays, and poems we had just heard, fresh off the pen. To my amazement, the workshop came to life almost every meeting—not through my or Ian's will but through the faith and energy of the writers. It has been the participants who, for ten years, have continually created and sustained the workshop's reason for being. Why write? For the love, revelation, challenge, or amusement of it, that's why.

The routine of the workshop has changed little from its first years, except that now we meet at tables in the church's entryway, the narthex. The tenth year's group was unusually tight and cohesive, with several of the writers attending every session. Many were veterans of previous years' workshops, and it was they who gave the workshop its informal orderliness. In the early years, the workshop was like a bus traveling a long road, with folks hopping on for a stop or two or three. In 2004, we traveled the main road together, with instructors Ian Frazier, Susan Shapiro, and myself taking turns with the driving and navigating.

The participants, however, are as always the stars, and we hope they continue to write for themselves and for the workshop in the years to come. Their stories, tragic and comic, of trials and revelations, of despair and inspiration, have been shared bravely and honestly. For this they have our admiration, love, and gratitude.

Part 1:

—

Who, Where, How?

Where I'm From

Carol West
March 31, 2004

I was the only fat one in my Virginia family. It's the fault of my grand-mother Eck's great southern cooking. I still wear her mashed potatoes and hand-beaten biscuits. I have hourglass hips and a pear-shaped ass. People notice.

Trying to find clothes to fit that bundle of love area is a challenge. Due to my short stature, I take into consideration first length, then width. Then the eye judges the style, the fabric, the color and design. The final question mentally asked before entering the dressing room is WILL IT FIT?

If it fits or might fit, do I look decent? If I look okay, the next concern is will I be able to find a seamstress or tailor who does good work at a cheap price to alter the item? If it fairly fits and looks okay, I buy it.

This season a pair of sexy silk-like, black Vietnamese pajama pants has served me well. For the afternoon, I add a business jacket. Perhaps a glittery top for an evening soiree. My outfit, in the winter, is black jeans or a pair of navy blue cords. Summer brings me khaki shorts. I have no shame. A bad day for a garment worker who makes mistakes can be a wonderfully fitting day for me.

Grandma Eck, you cooked too well.

Where I Am From

Peter Nkruma
March 26, 2003

I am from Uganda, the eye of the skull-shaped African continent. And from the eye I am. The lush, hot African landscape receded and a Canadian one took its place in my life. Cold, long winters and free roaming wolf-dog hybrids as numerous as snowflakes were my morning. Then in the afternoon, the Canadian canvas was replaced with an American one. Washington serenaded me with star-spangled anthems as I ate hot apple pie at the ballgame. But as the twilight fell, the ghosts of all the dead Indians roamed in the growing darkness, like the wolf dogs of Canada, and the lions of Africa. The ghosts of the Indians found their way onto this page.

Where I'm From

Norman Clayton
March 10, 2004

Love, rage, fear: all come to me this dawn. But let me start with love, which circles around me like the electronic ticker tapes here in Times Square.

Love. It too advances and retreats, turns corners, tells of victory and defeat. Love was never mentioned in my family; love was almost taboo. I never saw my mother and father hug and kiss. When my mother got pregnant with my older brother, a deal was made. My father would work, she would cook, clean, and take care of the kids. That was it, that was the marriage. "That's it," was Pop's letter signoff. I remember his handwriting. He slashed the T's of "That's it" vertically and horizontally like the sunlight on the ground in New York City. I am mentally ill, so it is sometimes nice to be on the ground and in sunlight.

Rage. When I was twelve, my cousin and I were walking down the hill near Trevose, Pennsylvania, when we saw a woman evangelist with a table full of palm-sized, shiny black books. They were copies of the New Testament. She said that if we took Christ as our savior, we could each have a Bible. My cousin wanted one. I didn't, but I went along with him and pledged Christ as my savior. It was the first time I saw my cousin, who was one year older, interested in anything but football and sex. My Bible was soon lost, but I remember its words of sin with their fiery glow. It was a sunny morning, the pages were tissue thin and almost translucent. Christ was in black type but Satan almost jumped off the page. I thought if my cousin wanted it, it must be sex. Christ didn't seem to be getting any, but Satan sure as hell was.

Fear. At home, though we were not holy rollers, my father was a devout follower of our small-town Elks Club. My mother, when I was in my mid-teens, chaired a Presbyterian women's organization. She asked me to get confirmed, so I did. She never said, "I'm proud of you." But thirty years later she finally started ending our telephone conversations with "Love and miss."

Where I'm From

Donald Mackey
February 1, 1995

1942 Born in Winston Salem, North Carolina.

1944 I remember my father throwing a piece of paper sprayed with quinine into my crib for the purpose of stopping my paper-eating habit. It worked. I started pulling wallpaper from the wall to chew on.

1945 I stood at a window in my house watching the rain flow down the street where I lived. It looked like a ferocious river carrying debris of tree limbs and other scary things. I cried for hours because I imagined that my mother might have been caught in the flood. She had gone to work.

1946 First day of Sunday school.

1949 First day at school. I still remember what I wore.

1955 Began high school.

1958 Moved to New Jersey.

1963 Married.

1966 My father died.

1966 First child born.

1966 Entered college.

1967 First professional employment.

1968 Reentered college.

1978 Purchased a home.

1989 Filed for bankruptcy.

1990 Drug rehab program.

1993 Became homeless.

1993 Wrote book manuscript.

1993 Became gainfully employed.

1994 Job closed.

1994 Became homeless again.

1995 Still homeless, looking for housing.

Where I'm From

Nelson Blackman
March 7, 2001

My mother, Lillie, was from Alabama. She had caramel skin, a round, pretty face and long dark hair, a southern belle. My father Harry was from New Orleans. He had mixed blood, part Cajun, part African American, part Cherokee. He was six feet four inches, one inch taller than me. He was married before meeting my mother and had three sons. They were already grown when I was born. I liked having three older brothers to look up to. We're close to this day. My parents had two daughters before me, so I was the baby.

I grew up in a tenement house on a quiet block on 128th Street in Harlem. My father was strict and made me go to Catholic school. He worked as a merchant seaman, so he traveled a lot. We missed him. Later he took a job with the phone company, which was better because he was home more. I loved trains when I was a kid. When he took me on the subway, I was mesmerized with the way it came out of the ground.

My father died in September of 1986. I visited his grave in New Jersey once with my brother. My mother died in April of 2001. She's buried in Calverton Cemetery in Long Island. I was closer to her. I went to her grave and talked to her, thanking her for taking such good care of me. For the last ten years of their marriage, my parents went their separate ways, which is why they are not buried together.

Where I'm From

Janice English
March 28, 2001

I come from a very dysfunctional family. There were six children. My father was physically abusive. He was emotionally and mentally abusive to my mother, and she was abusive to us as well.

This is where fear starts and you become scared all the time; scared if you did something wrong, scared if you didn't do anything wrong. You never know in this type of situation what kind of mood your parents are in that would incite them to beat you. So you lived in fear and were afraid all the time. Being scared becomes a way of life. Because society makes you think that you have no rights until you are eighteen, you sometimes buy into this crap.

My father started heavily abusing me when I was twelve, and it lasted for six years. I went into junior high school weighing 112 pounds. By the time I finished the ninth grade I was 160 pounds. I came out in the twelfth grade weighing 180 pounds. During these years, he abused me for no reason. He didn't want me talking to boys. He used to accuse me of everything under the sun, though it was all in his head. I was scared all the time. I had no protection, no one I could talk to. So I used to eat and run away from home all the time.

When I turned eighteen, my mother got the courage to separate from my father. He used to come to where we lived and break the door down or climb through the window and terrorize us. At eighteen I felt like an adult and didn't want to take this anymore. So one day when he broke into the house and hit me, I hit him back. I even broke my high school graduation picture over his head. We had a knockdown, drag-out fight. We broke the bed and some furniture and to be honest with you I never had any trouble out of him since that day. He never laid a hand on me again.

If I hadn't been so scared all those years, I would have avoided a lot of pain. But I grew up in a time where we had respect for our mothers and fathers. You did not question their authority. Today I find most people live in fear and are afraid all the time. I try not to deal with those types of people. Yet I have compassion for them because I was scared in the past. But guess what? I'm not scared anymore.

Where I Come From

Walter Schubert
March 26. 2003

Since I'm always on my way, going someplace, a better question is "Where are you coming from?"

T. S. Eliot started out by saying, "In my end is my beginning." There is much work that I still have to do before I accept my end. I would work to make myself a useful citizen of this country. I have much to offer, and much of what I have to offer is in what I have to say.

It is not that I am full of myself. Yet I believe that many of the problems that America is facing are not unlike the personal problems I have. America might do well to lend me her ear to see how I have succeeded where I find her to be faltering.

It is not as though what I have to say has already been said by others. I am different from the people around me. Social workers try to deal with me by looking up the answer in the back of the book. They do not understand that their book is the wrong book. The right book has not yet been written.

Yes, I was born in New York City, on December 17, 1942. It was ten days after Enrico Fermi's achievement of controlled fission. It was Beethoven's birthday. It was the middle of the World War. Music, science, and history are in my blood. Their fundamental precepts are the context in which I stand in this instant of time's momentum. They are the horizon that surrounds me in everything I hope to do.

On the seashore I see what I can reach for: a land of acceptance and welcome. A journey that began when my parents left Europe is finding its place in America, just as America is finding her place in the world. My role is to add significance to what she does. We hear overtones, for music is an international language.

In the end, we two have much left to say.

My Name and How I Got It

Norman B. Clayton
March 8, 2000

No, my birth certificate does not say Normie. Norm and Normie, except for family members, is a no-no. My birth certificate says May 23, 1939, Norman Boyd Clayton was born.

That's the important part. My mother named me—that's an important part too. She thought Norman was a regal name. She thought me regal too. I have run away from Norman the name and Norman the person. I went with "Clay" for a while, short for my last name. That started in the army where everyone has their last name on their uniform.

I was even a halfway hippie for a while as "Clay," not that I was trying to get away from mom's good wishes. Regal? Norman seemed effeminate, and I wanted no part of that. It took me several visits to mental institutions to get away from "Clay" and from Norman.

But that's another story. You can call me Norman, especially if you're buying me lunch.

Where I Got My Name From

Thyatira English
March 21, 2001

Everybody always asks where my name is from. I really don't like to tell people where it's from, but I'll tell you today.

I'm named after one of the seven churches in the Bible. See, I love my name so much that I tell people the wrong way to say it, because I don't want them to know the right way. My name is that special.

My first name means daughter. My middle name, Sayyida, means happiness. They mean such great things that I don't want anyone else to have them or know.

My Name and How I Got It

Damita Boston
March 3, 2004

The name is Dee. Not Dee exactly, but much easier to pronounce than Damita. Not many people are familiar with the name except for a few *Solid Gold* fans. You see, *Solid Gold* was this old dance show that came on television like a disco *Soul Train*. The main female "Solid Golder" was this chick named Damita Jo, consequently stirring some type of familiarity with the name in people of my mother's age group, old timers, coke bangers, boxed wine drinkers, and pimps. Ha!

Nevertheless, this scantily clad rump shaker of the '70s show *Solid Gold* was not the lucky woman for whom I was named. Much like everything about me, my name in itself is also very weird. Damita is actually accompanied by a small appendage—Asa Damita. Asa means "nubile lady of the morning," a derivative of the old Spaniard language. The latter is none other than Japanese. Now I'm done showing off my knowledge of unimportant words in other languages.

My Name and How I Got It

Carol West
April 19, 2000

My parents decided that if I had been a boy my mother would name me. I was a girl, so my father named me: Carol Ann. I hated the name from earliest memory. Carol Annnnnn, a two-syllable southern moniker that spoke on forever. When talked about I became "little" Carol Ann.

I wanted to be Caroline after my grandmother Caroline, but my Aunt Mary joined a religious order and became Sister Caroline. There would not be three Carolines in my family.

I wanted to be a Caroline. My life would have been better. I would have been happier. I would have been taller, slimmer, and prettier. I could have been snotty Caroline, uppity Caroline, even smart-assed Caroline. I just wanted to be a Caroline with a different numerology, a different vibration, maybe creating a different attitude.

I tried with my confirmation name, but Sister Edwina wasn't going for Carol Ann Caroline, so I became Carol Ann Mary . . . sigh.

Carol Ann was just a name screamed at me, repeated regretfully by my elders or spoken with disappointment. Tack on to Carol Ann my Swiss family name Roesle from the German-speaking canton near Bern, and you have a mouthful. Roesle means "little rose," and no one ever pronounced or wrote Roesle right. Carol Ann "little rose." Oh please.

Sometimes I think I married Mr. West just for his name. Now I'm Carol West. It's generic, it's simple, it's easy to remember, and it's just me.

How I Got My Name

Jeff Rubin
March 21, 2001

It's funny you should ask that question. I am an Ashkenazi Jew. We of the Ashkenazi name after the dead, whereas the Sephardic name after the living. Both are equal and have their own strengths. My Jewish name is *Yisrael Yedah* or Jeffrey J. I was named after my *Zaddi's* (grandfather in Yiddish) brother, who was lost in the Holocaust. I think it is a brilliant tradition to name a child after the dead. You get a sense of immortality—like the deceased donor giving his organs to the living.

You have to remember that you are never really dead until you are forgotten. By naming after the dead, you are always remembered. I remember talking to my *Bubbi* (grandmother in Yiddish). She was telling a story of how her firstborn son, Borichel, was killed as a three-year-old back in the old country of Galicia, which exists no more. A horse and wagon ran over him when he was running across the street to meet my grandparents. He was my mother's brother. He would have been my uncle. He would have been in his eighties with grandchildren of his own possibly. Alas, he remains a three-year-old for all of eternity.

I wanted to name my first son after him. My grandmother said no. Why? She said, "It didn't bring him luck, so what makes you think it will bring your son any?" So Borichel would remain dead, or so I thought.

I had dinner at an Orthodox Jewish home this past Purim. Going to *shul*, I overheard the mother of the home turn to her husband and say, "We have to find Borichel. We can't leave without him." My ears could not believe what they had just heard. I said, "What? What did you say? About Borichel?"

She said he was her son, and that they could not leave without him. I smiled, and she looked at me strangely. "Why?" the woman asked.

I said it was a long story and that I would tell her on the way over to the *shul*. I thought, "Thank God, Borichel has a name. He would no longer be a three-year-old. He would grow up to be a husband and father with grandchildren of his own." Borichel lives!

My Name and How I Got It

Mitch Wiater
March 8, 2000

My father has my first name, my father's father had my name also, and maybe my grandfather's father had the same name, but I'm not sure. My father, who is eighty-two years old, does not remember. My oldest son got my name, and maybe his first son will get the name too.

It means time in the past, present, and the future. It means continuing traditions.

When I came to America from Poland, my first name MIECZYSLAW was too difficult for people to say. They called me MIECZ, MICHELL, and MICHAEL. So I changed it to Mitch. I still have a problem with my last name Wiater, which very often is written and pronounced "Waiter."

How I Came to New York

Nelson Blackman
March 15, 2000

My parents are from the South, but they met while they were both living in the Bronx. I was born here, at Syndehen Hospital at 122nd Street and St. Nicholas Avenue. It's not there anymore. Mayor Koch turned it into an old folks' home. I was born the same day that the famous jazz singer Dinah Washington died—December 15, 1963.

Living in Harlem was pretty easy, but the heavy traffic, subway delays, and crowded sidewalks can get a person's nerves worked up. When I was thirteen, my mother took me to see my Aunt Rebecca in Birmingham, Alabama. She had a big house, with lots of food and relatives, but it was hot and boring there. I got homesick for the city that never sleeps. I missed the subways and buses and noise. In the South, people were so laid back. Everything was too slow. In New York there's always something to do.

How I Got to New York

Tory Connolly Walker
March 3, 2004

I got to New York by default. I had made several trips to visit but living here was by happenstance.

The first time I got a glimpse of this fabulous city, I was visiting as a post-debutante, pre-college student, an eighteen-year-old, wide-eyed ingénue with life stretched before me like a golden brick road. New York was just like I pictured it: Big. Bad. Dramatic. I stayed at the Iroquois Hotel on 44th Street—two doors down from the Algonquin. I peered through those hallowed windows imagining I was a celebrated reporter/writer in a '40s-style hat with a wicked tilt. It was the '70s, but I dressed with a '40s flair—tailored suits, seamed stockings, open-toed heels, an upswept hairdo with a cascade of curls above the brow. I fancied myself just like New York. Big. Bold. Bad. Dramatic. Yet as bad as I wanted to be, New York scared me, and I scurried back home to Ohio after my two-week visit.

Fast-forward to age twenty-four. My second visit to the city was more as a young sophisticate. I had a college degree in hand, and two years of work as a news reporter in Columbus giving me a more confident, almost cocky walk. I had come with my cousin who was vacationing. I, on the other hand, was job hunting. Still we did the city in spectacular style. My cousin, who worked for an airline, was just as bombastic as I, so we both knew how to "live large" on a budget.

She got half-price fare on hotels, and half of that (with us sharing the room) suddenly made the amazing Park Plaza on Fifth Avenue affordable. We became instant snobs. Dining in the Russian Tea Room, riding the horse-drawn carriages through Central Park, tipping bellboys (and detaining the cute ones), going to Studio 54—and being turned down! We were aghast. Came back to the hotel mirror to look at ourselves in black dresses and shiny black heels and decided we weren't wild enough, funky enough, and "heroin chic" looking enough to be picked for that stupid ol' Studio 54. I looked for a job at NBC and the Sheridan Broadcasting Network, where I landed an interview but not the job. My cousin noticed at nights I drank to excess and often needed a drink in the morning. Of course, she drank and got giggly herself. Little did I know the clutch of alcohol was sinking its talons deep within.

My fourth trip to New York was different from my heady Park Plaza days. I was thirty-eight years old, had one marriage in L.A. behind me, and a second husband in L.A. from whom I was separated. I ran to New York with my alcohol and drug counselor to get away from it all. Yet I was not getting away but hauling a truckload of ghost baggage with me.

By that time I not only had an alcohol habit but a powder and crack cocaine habit, had lost my reporting career, and had been hospitalized over twenty-two times for manic-depression. Big. Bad. Dramatic. New York I hardly knew "ye." But the Lord would set me free.

How I Came to New York

Carol West
March 21, 2001

I lived in San Francisco for six months in 1979, when my husband was renting a seat on the Stock Exchange. Anything that could go wrong, did. The wind off the Bay never stopped, and I always had to wear a heavy sweater. To paraphrase Mark Twain, the coldest summer I ever spent was my entire stay in San Francisco.

That year was there was a gas shortage nationwide and instead of visiting outlying areas, you sat in your car for hours in gas lines. For short drives to the beach or up the coast, if you had gas, you couldn't find a parking space. My husband did not spend money. Not on eating out. No handicrafts or magnificent bottles of California wine. We drank water at zero cost.

I lived on New York time in California. My husband was at the exchange by seven a.m. and left at one p.m. when his day was over. We went to sleep at nine o'clock at night. I was always thinking ahead three hours. I dreamed of the East Coast.

We lived in a nice little garden apartment that many people mistook for the super's place. My bell was always ringing. We averaged one earthquake a month. One night while I watched TV on the futon, the floor gently shook. It was like touching a bowl of Jell-O—1.5 on the Richter scale. It was the last straw.

I got up, packed everything, sold our furniture, and within three days was ready to move back to Manhattan—with or without my husband. He saw how serious I was and started packing our cream-colored Camero. We left at four the next morning, the last thing we did on California time.

How I Came to New York

Jay Stockman
March 3, 2004

I'm from Harrington Park, New Jersey. Like many people I wanted a better life, and education seemed the way to get it. I arranged to stay with relatives in the Bronx near a subway line, leading me to a nearby graduate school. After a short time studying occupational therapy at NYU, I (maybe foolishly) transferred majors (to sociology).

Classes led me to explore such community groups as the Chelsea Coalition and Metropolitan Council on Housing. I became involved with the Catholic Worker. It exists today, though some may argue its original mission changed as our world has altered.

After coming to New York my life has gone through many changes, but what brought me here has not. You might say that this soup kitchen is an outgrowth of my early idealism tempered by reality.

How I Got to New York

Jeff Rubin
March 3, 2004

Easy—I was conceived here. I am a native New Yorker, son of Jewish immigrant parents who came to America back in the 1920s and settled on the Lower East Side. They were originally from a country called Galicia, located on the southern part of the Carpathian Mountains and part of the Austro-Hungarian Empire. Do not try to find it because it exists no more. It has been broken up in a million pieces after the First World War in which my grandfather fought and was wounded very badly, losing most of his hearing. Today Galicia's north is part of Poland, its middle became part of Ukraine, and its southern part became Romania. I guess that's what you get when you have Franz-Joseph as your emperor. In 1992 I went back to Austria to find my roots and to look for my uncle Borichel's grave. To my surprise when I got there I found out that we really were not Austrians at all, just ruled by them. By the way, Galicia is in Bram Stoker's *Dracula*. But he got his location wrong. Dracula's castle is actually in the southern part of Romania and exists today.

How I Came to New York

Mitch Wiater
March 15, 2000

The first time I came to New York was over seven years ago, for tourism on a visa. I wanted to visit family and friends here. The first time I stayed in New York almost nine months, trying to see as much as possible. But I could not see everything. I was limited by time and money.

After I visited friends in America and Canada, my visa expired. I returned to my family in Poland. Then my wife got mail from the United States Embassy in Poland, informing her that she, her husband and children had won a green card lottery. It surprised her. During my visit I had sent in the application but did not tell her about it. A couple of months later, we arrived in New York. We stayed ten months this time.

We rented an apartment, where the landlord didn't allow for anything. We didn't have hot water. Our sons couldn't speak too loudly. They couldn't think about playing in the apartment because the landlord lived below and always said, "Don't be so noisy," adding that we had to find another apartment soon. It was too expensive, and my younger son Adan missed his friends in Poland.

After my wife and two sons returned to Poland, I stayed in New York, trying to find a job and improve my English. I love New York. I took special computer classes. After I found a job and saved money, my family came back and joined me. Now I am not sure they can stay for good, because one month ago I lost the job. Now it's a full-time job looking for another job.

How I Came to New York City

Pierce McLoughlin
March 15, 2000

I came to New York City through St. Vincent's Hospital on September 26, 1944. I did not have too much choice in the matter. Tragically my parents' marriage was a disaster. My mom was born in this country and had a college education. Fortunately I took after her side of the family.

My father, while basically a good man, had little or no respect for education and even less respect for God (Catholic Church/Cardinal Spellman 1950–1960). He was a good salesman and worked for Krug Bakers in Westchester as a route man.

We had a seven-and-a-half-room apartment on Riverside Drive, near Grant's Tomb ($140.00 per month). However, my parents lived virtually separate lives for 20 years in separate bedrooms.

Mom was a writer in America. She worked as a freelancer. She died of cancer in 1967. She instilled in us a love of God and schooling. Without her my brother, sister, and I would have fallen apart. Dad lived and died as a functional alcoholic, unrepentant to the end. He died in Ireland with his second wife in 1995.

As you might guess, I also developed as an alcoholic but had enough insight and discipline to stop the booze (October 18, 1979). Today I have twenty years of sobriety. I started out in life to be a priest. Ironically, I've probably heard more confessions in my twelve-step program.

Father's Day

Carol West
May 7, 2003

My parents were divorced. I don't remember seeing my father until I was eleven. First of the month, every month, there was a payment of $30. My father gave cash to my Swiss immigrant grandfather, who had my grandmother mail the check to my mother. Upon receipt, my mother would wail that $30 never went very far with clothes, school-books, and medical expenses. Thirty dollars was spit up in a down-wind.

Once my father saw me, childcare was upped $15 more. I was sent to Catholic boarding school hoping they could "do something with me." I started to get a card at Christmas and my birthday with $10 in it, and if I was lucky a note. One year I was taken to Virginia Beach with my stepmother and two younger siblings to stay with my father's family. I didn't fit in or behave in his accepted way and was not invited back. My father did not invite me to holiday gatherings or my grandfather's funeral. I found out on my own about his death and attended, to my father's dismay.

On the first of the month after my eighteenth birthday the money stopped. The indiscretion of a young, bad marriage had been paid off, in full. I last saw my father twenty-three years ago. He had inappropriate things to say to me about my mother. Who was he to point a finger? I have not spoken to him since. I don't know if he's alive or dead. Happy Father's Day.

He Was Like a Father to Me

Tory Connolly Walker
March 10, 2004

My father, my flesh-and-blood DNA daddy, was like a father to me, because he was my father—but more so. He was a gift. Truly, no embellishment. The world's fathers aren't all fatherly. Some are just babies' daddies, some are deadbeats, some detached, others invisible. The worst are the abusive, unrepentant ones.

Quésnel A. Connolly Jr., they called him Q.A., was a gift—a balm to my psyche, memory, and troubled soul. After my having lived through as an adult a truckload of terror and trauma, a boatload of mojos and curses. After spending years trying to hack through a mile-thick wall of demons and devils only to fall in a heap at my Heavenly Father's feet, I am blessed. The real blessing was that for an achingly short time, I had an earthly father who was special. Godly, kind, intelligent, authoritative, wise, and fatherly. That was Daddy. That's why it may come as a shock when I say he was schizophrenic. A Korean War veteran, former high school science teacher, and a diagnosed, paranoid, card-carrying schizophrenic.

Mental illness runs in families. The remarkable thing is that he managed to be a rock to me even with his illness. He was still kind, intelligent, and I was Daddy's girl. We went to zoos, libraries, museums, and movies. As a child I scarcely knew there was anything wrong with my father. It was all hush-hush, such a stigma. Mental illness was whispered then shushed up when I bounded my little girl self into the room where adult family members had congregated.

My mother and father were separated, and I often stayed with my grandmother. Besides being super superstitious, she had her own kind of anxious, worried love towards me. Rabbit foots, salt thrown over the shoulder, no hats on the bed, fussy lucky charm, here's a four-leaf clover love. One day Daddy was late. I waited at Mama Harry's house (my nickname for my grandmother), and we both peered nervously out the parlor window. I twirled the leaves off a four-leaf clover. Finally, he arrived—apparently after a doctor's visit.

I hugged him happily and he hugged me back, then slowly, matter-of-factly said, "Tory, I'm not taking you on our outing today."

"Why not?" I asked sadly.

"Daddy's sick," he said.

"Where does it hurt?" I asked.

"My head—my brain to be exact. I'm a sick, sick man."

"Your brain?" I asked in six-year-old puzzlement.

My father looked at me through tortoise-shell glasses as his eyes became pools of sadness. He collapsed on the couch in a giant six-foot-four-inch heap, suddenly looking like a tiny baby. He wailed like I'd never seen him. "Oh, Tory," he said. "Mental illness is a terrible, terrible thing."

Mental illness. There. I'd heard it from Daddy's mouth himself. That dreaded, awful thing everyone whispered. The huge reason my Daddy and Mommy were no longer married. Why he lost his job as a beloved high school science teacher. Why he was on disability. Why we couldn't all be a family. Why Mommy was remarrying. Why? I asked that question many times throughout the years.

One day it wasn't me staring in the square window of the metal door of a mental hospital—at my forlorn father's face. One day it was me as a twenty-four-year-old woman staring out through that square window—at my visitors. My dear father, through mental illness and freedom and back to the veterans' hospital again, would tell me, "Tory, read your Bible, honey. I believe you can get free." Daddy believed in Jesus, and he passed on his belief to me. Sadly, he did not know how to get himself free.

My Father

Thyatira English
April 10, 2002

I heard through the grapevine that my father had passed away. It was very emotional, especially since I was only fourteen years old. He died on my nephew's birthday, which was strange.

When my brother came knocking on the door, I opened it. When I saw his face, I knew my father had died. The thing that I know most was that he had been suffering, and he was now in a better place.

I never went to his funeral. I don't regret that. I didn't go because he's watching me everywhere I go. I heard through the grapevine that my father is happy and not suffering anymore.

His Face

Donald Mackey
April 16, 1997

My father was a very loving man. Yet he was the sternest man I ever knew. He had a big grin, though he seldom grinned. When he did, he seemed to be making up for the times that he didn't. The muscles in his face seemed stretched to the limit.

My dad laughed only at his own jokes. He would roll over laughing, while my sisters, my brother, and I looked at each other. We feigned laughter. I never thought that his jokes were funny at all.

After my father died, I studied the last photograph he had taken. I discovered that I was really seeing his face for the first time—the warm eyes, the shape of his nose and how shiny it was, the rough line of checks from years of shaving, the stern mouth. How peaceful he looked.

The Worst Mother's Day

Carol West
April 17, 2002

I always hated Mother's Day. My rearing was left to other people, but when the day came around, I really couldn't understand why you had to be nice to "the mother" who knowingly, in the wink of an eye, could be "out to lunch" in my life.

I was passed around to relatives because of illness and alcoholism in my family. I was made aware that I "didn't fit in." At nine, for my own good, I was packed off to Catholic boarding school. I have had problems with Mother Superior authority figures ever since.

On Mother's Day, my mother expected diffidence, gifts, and due respect on my part. I got the card and the gift to acknowledge the day. My mother's life was all about *her* young successes, *her* failures, and *her* yesterdays. Her one accomplishment was having me, I was always reminded.

On Mother's Day, when females over sixteen years of age are wished a Happy Mother's Day, I hate it. I never had any children, never wanted to be a mother. The woman who was labeled "Mother," who I am sure meant well, never showed me how to nurture or relate. No one wants to talk about the dark side of Mother's Day. I wish the day would just go away.

Worst

Norman Clayton
March 31, 2004

Time was a river
I floated on without grace
Just gambling
Isolated, insulated, me, me, me.
My mother was gone
And I honestly don't remember
       me me me
One single
Mother's Day good
Or bad, just ten years of
Horses, and horse racing
That I remember.
But that's gone now, 155 days clean
Like my mother was clean
And who would now be proud of me.

The Worst Mother's Day

Tory Connolly Walker
March 31, 2004

I love my mother, but we've been estranged for over a year now. My last telephone exchange with her was last February. I love my mother, but I wonder how many Americans can proudly use that expression for a dysfunctional relationship. I love my mother, but . . . she just drives me nuts. The last time she left a message on my voice mail was February 9, 2003, and I didn't return her call. I'd never done that before. Didn't have the guts, gumption, or audacity. After all, I'm a Bible-believing woman and right up there in the Ten Commandments is "Honor thy mother and father." Maybe I should call her soon. Just to not tick off God. Why haven't I called her or seen her a year? I just can't psychically process her behavior anymore without pain.

Here's a scene from "The Worst Mother's Day Ever." It was Mother's Day 1998. As always, I was prepared to send my mother a nice Hallmark greeting, for $3.50. I don't know about most moms, but when my mom's done reading the flowery message (and my funny comments designed to pluck a petal or two off the rosy prose), she always flips the card over to check how much I coughed up to pay for her greeting. It never seems to be enough, so I usually overcompensate by buying two cards and sending a gift.

I thought I'd do something really special for Mumsy this year. I'd send her a gift and a living card. I'd make one myself. Since Mother's Day always falls on a Sunday, I'd take off Friday morning and give her a live greeting two days early.

That's right. "Live on television." Not just any television— national television. Not just any show, the *Today* morning news program outside, when they scan the audience. So I spent four hours the night before working diligently on her card. Since my sister was a mama's girl and lived within shouting distance of her in Columbus, Ohio, I put a picture of my mom, my sister, and me on it with the phrase, "Mom, you're one in a million!" Truer words were never spoken. It was glitterized and gold letterized and big, bold, and flamboyant (but not flowery).

I showed the card to a neighbor, my good friend Ray-Ray. He shook his head sadly like an old sage. "I hope she appreciates it." Ray-Ray, now deceased, had a tenuous hold on life, having kidney disease and enduring daily dialysis. He appreciated everything. "I'd get a kick out of it," he said, "but I don't know about your mother."

I got up at the crack of dawn to get a good spot by the *Today* show rope at Rockefeller Center—somewhere conspicuous where I could get right in Al Roker's face and grab the national spotlight for a few seconds. I called my mom right before the show to let her know I'd be on the *Today Show* segment from 7:25 until 8:00ish. She said, "Really?" in her not surprised, but I-wonder-why-on-earth way.

I was already crestfallen, but I got up a big grin for the camera and yelled like any other nutty tourist. (I wasn't a tourist. I live in New York.) I needed camera time and attention to make my Mother's Day special, and I got it. I screamed and waved my huge greeting card each time the camera made a swoop, and Al gave the weather in his irreverent-weather-guy style. Finally at 8:30 I called my mother (who worked as an executive and set her own hours) to ask her if she'd seen my live greeting. "Mom, did you see me? Did you see your card?"

"What? Oh," she said. "I had to find some pantyhose and I think I missed you, Tory."

This time I was beyond crestfallen. I was devastated. "Did you tell Shell (my sister) to watch it?" I asked, just as hurt by her as I was at five, seven, nine, eleven, seventeen, and beyond.

"Shell has to go to work," my mother snapped. (My sister also had a great job and did not punch a clock.)

"Oh," I said. I got up two days and three hours early to give her a live greeting. "I see," I said, trying not to sound so little-girl hurt. "Happy Mother's Day then."

"Okay. Thanks," said my mother. "Oh, that's my boyfriend, Milton. I have to go."

"I'll let you go then, Mom," I said feeling alone. "Talk to you later."

"I will never call that woman again!" I screamed in Rockefeller Center. Tourists looked at me like another New Yorker had snapped. I went to a deli to get coffee. Hands shaking, I got the key to the ladies restroom and locked myself in and heaved huge sobs for twenty minutes. Finally, I got myself together enough to call Ray-Ray. He said, "Yeah, I was afraid of that." Then I called Chuckie, my photographer friend back in Columbus. "That's a dog-gone shame," he said.

Good. I was not just being oversensitive. I smoothed my hair, straightened my blouse, and put on lipstick to face the faceless in New York, which suddenly didn't seem so cold. I smiled. A lady smiled back. Yes, the cold front was in Ohio. New York was sunny, hopeful, warm.

My Mother

Jay Stockman
April 21, 2004

My father, a machine salesman, passed away in 1963. Then a huge car wreck I was in five months later, when I was seventeen, did further damage to me and my family. The immediate effect was weeks of unconsciousness. Neurological problems were not yet evident. I was lucky almost beyond belief to have such a resourceful, persistent, and loving mother in charge of my care. Taking care of me was difficult, but she seemed to get stronger doing it. She took a job doing billing for a trucking company. She hunted down medical resources that I needed, which was not easy at the time.

She was a tall, pretty woman with black hair, from an Episcopalian family. She passed away in 2001 from senile dementia. I worry that I never quite wound up doing as well as she'd intended.

At Seventeen

Peter Nkruma
April 30, 2003

When I was seventeen I wrote constantly. My dream was to be a novelist like Dostoevski or Anne Rice. My favorite book was *Candide*, by Voltaire, and I thought Plato's *Dialogues* were the cleverest invention of all time.

I listened to classical music and heavy metal and hip-hop. My favorite hobby was chasing girls. I painted vague images of Greek women in watercolors, wrote bad but sincere poetry, and read omnivorously.

I interned in the offices of a Brooklyn city councilwoman. The work was rewarding and gave me a sense of authority. At seventeen I was a breezy, fun kid. I thought I knew everything. Now, of course, looking back, I hardly knew a thing. Still, if I met me at seventeen now, I wouldn't mind having a beer with me.

At Seventeen

Donald Mackey
April 2, 1997

My mother allowed me to have my seventeenth birthday party with my brother, sisters, and our friends while she had to work. I lived on Clifton Avenue between Park and 7th Avenues. Our apartment building was directly across the street from Sacred Heart Cathedral; I think it is said to be the third largest cathedral in the world. Pope John Paul II once visited the church when he was in New York.

The party got out of hand when a boy who happened to belong to a gang accused another gang member of dancing too close with his girlfriend. The accused drew a knife and held it pointed at the accuser. The accuser grabbed the blade of the knife and dared the accused to cut his hand. The accused snatched the blade back toward him, cutting the hand of the accuser. Blood began to flow all over the white floral linoleum.

The boy who had the cut hand shouted that he was going to his neighborhood to bring back his members to my house. While he was away, my siblings and I put everyone out of the house. The two gang members had not been invited to the party.

After the gangs showed up at my house, they left peacefully seeing no one was there. My siblings and I managed to clean up all of the blood and straighten out the house by the time my mother came home from work. When she arrived we all sat around like little angels. The next morning the building's superintendent told her what had occurred. My mother said no more parties when she wasn't at home.

Seventeen

Carol West
March 19, 1997

When I was seventeen
I can still feel the pain
Of failure
Of loneliness
Of joy not coming my way
Of rock and riot and not
Being there
Of Berkeley and hanging
Loose. I'd lose control
Of my nothing world.
There was still embarrassment
In wrong choices: Don't do this.
My family: The hoped-for mold
Of a Southern Cinderella.

Of not understanding the beginning
Of the obscenity of 'Nam
Of being impotent to do anything
About anything
Of not speaking out.

I see them acting out, Seeger, Dylan,
And James Baldwin. They had a new ethic
Down the road of now.
A boy would look at me and
I'd gain five pounds. My face a pool of oil
Over-manufacturing blackheads.

I was not the chosen one, ever.
Grandma got me a generic
Anonymous prom date that
June night
A year of failure
When I was seventeen,
Of going nowhere in reverse.

My First Love

Donald Mackey
February 22, 1995

Linda was my first love. I was sixteen years of age, and she was twelve. Knowing that it would have been improper to be with her intimately, with great restraint I settled for hiding behind the stairwell to kiss. Linda was very mature for her age. It was because of Linda that I began to think seriously about my future job security. When Linda's family moved away a year and a half later, I was heartbroken. I didn't know where she was. Linda's personality served for many years as the measuring rule by which I chose my female friends. The big difference was that Linda had initially come on to me. But now it seemed that I had to do the approaching. Even though I had my fair share of female friends, I had told myself that the one I could really fall in love with would be the one who found me or noticed me first.

Because of our age differences we never spoke openly in public. We had it arranged where she called me on the phone, but I could not call her because that would make me suspect. I used to sit on the front stoop and watch her play. She was always the leader of the group. She was intelligent. She was pretty. I just believed that she was all these things naturally. I thought she was too young to be consciously trying to impress me.

I ran into Linda forty-two years later. I was standing on a street corner waiting to cross the street. The meeting was ecstatic. She was divorced, and so was I. We dated, had sex. I dropped my guard.

It was Linda who turned me on to cocaine. My life has never been the same.

First Love

Norman Clayton
April 15, 2004

Eve, the trees itch, they always do
Grounded fruit calling to you,
Always to you, to lonely you,
Woman who had no choice
I climb down almost the first time.

It is still not too late to get lost.
Let me sip you with a cup of wine,
White wine me, white wine you
Always longing and calling
Moonless always lovelorn you.

First Love

Paul Coleman
April 16, 1997

She looks just like
That woman I love,
Always have

When she was younger
She was supine, effervescent,
Witty and classy

I've seen all her movies,
Know where she lives,
Know all about her

She walks just like
A dancer from the
Australian Ballet Company

I'm smitten, been bitten,
Ain't quitting until we're one again.
I've had her. I've lost her.

She acts just like six good years
Of my life, lived like man and wife
Is gone now, is memories

I was her Spencer Tracy

My First Love

Carol West
April 26, 2000

I've always been aware of my first love. For all the loves who have come in and through my life, who I've loved intensely and sweetly, this love remains. For men who have loved me and left or those who have had the door shut in their face. None has ever touched me like my first love—food!

It's been a continuing affair since first memory, snacks at the circus. Grandmother always said I ate my way through the three rings. The terror of that day was holding the peanuts tightly fearing the elephant wanted one. I screamed scarlet and held the bag closer. I won. Dumbo was terrified.

I learned the art of cooking in my grandmother's southern kitchen. I did well there and had the weight to prove it. Food didn't talk back. Pork chops and fried apples, roast beef with mash and gravy. Home-canned veggies and preserves.

As I grew older I cooked my way into relationships and marriage. No one ever left my table and complained. As I fell out of love, I stopped cooking. Starve, baby, starve. I learned to prepare continental, Spanish, and Oriental cuisine. The nicest thing my former husband said about me was, "If you want to make Carol happy, just give her a cookbook."

In the war of weight, food won. Food loved me. People could see it, and I never said no to a box of chocolates. There's no "heroin chic" for me. Food is my comfort, my control, and the nicest reward. A new dish well prepared and enjoyed makes my endorphins sing.

It's a lifelong affair, and as you can see, I wear my love well.

My Best Mistake

Joe Negrelli
April 9, 2003

My best mistake was 7:30 Saturday morning on April 3, 1999. I awoke in the usual way with the clock radio going off at its normal time. I felt an abnormal malaise of unknown origin. However, I got up and started to do my normal chores. This feeling of discomfort did not abate but lingered without any additional symptoms.

After an hour of this I decided to lie down on my bed, but great pain and an overwhelming urge to urinate came over me. I ran to the bathroom and was surprised to see that I only peed a small amount. I washed my hands and was walking back to the bedroom still feeling extremely strange.

Then two steps out of the bathroom I thought I got punched by King Kong. One hit to the chest and I felt like all the air in my body was sucked out of me. Knowing that I couldn't call 911 myself, I jumped up to go get my neighbors to call an ambulance.

Thank goodness they were home. They told me they had called for an ambulance and to go downstairs to meet it. The pain receded as quickly as it had come. I took off to the street level. The ambulance only took a minute but it felt like hours. They drove me to the hospital and I was brought into the emergency room.

I asked the nurse for a pan to get sick in. Instead she brought me insurance forms. So being smart I decided to throw up on the floor. I knew I wasn't going to clean it up. The nurse brought a pan so I would feel better and asked an orderly to do an EKG on me right away.

As I watched the face of the orderly, dull as it was, I concluded that nothing was wrong due to lack of expression on his face. He tore off the paper and gave it to the doctor who ran up to me and said, "You're having a heart attack at this very moment."

I remember thinking he can tell me the truth. I can handle it. For the next twenty-one days they did tests and all types of procedures on me. The doctor said I needed open-heart surgery. Initially I strongly disagreed with him. Later I relented and they did a quadruple bypass.

The road to recovery has not yet hit the end, but I now thank the doctors (seven cardiologists, two cardiac surgeons, and one anesthesiologist) for their attentive work and kind hearts.

Best Mistake

Pierce McLoughlin
March 27, 2002

I was raised conservative Catholic. Irish Catholic. The days of
Cardinal Spellman and J. Edgar Hoover. I attended parochial schools
and was taught the proper behavior. God forbid you'd be seen in the
company of writers, especially secular writers in a Protestant church.
Hell fire was just around the corner for you.

Anyway, I behaved myself for thirty years, starting in 1950 and
graduated school on time. I finished college in New Mexico in 1967.
I joined the navy during Vietnam, not to be patriotic, to get away from
the Catholic Church. I went to Supply School and eventually to
Vietnam (1970). I was in the accounting section for the Pacex
Exchange System, got a field promotion to PO3, and came back to
the USA somewhat a hero.

After my discharge, I studied to be a priest but to no avail. After
six years (1973–1979) I was let go and returned to New York City
extremely depressed. I was a full-blown alcoholic after fourteen years
on the sauce. I chose to be the "thick Irish" man to the end. My best
mistake. Compliments of a Higher Power.

Back in New York, I looked for work, ignoring the warnings given
to me to go to AA. Finally, I gave up. I walked to the East River. After
drinking two bottles of vodka, jumped in. Enter the NYPD.

I spent ten weeks in a psych ward. I began going to twelve-step
meetings January 3, 1980. Twenty years later, I am still in twelve-step
groups. I've probably heard more confessions in recovery than I
would've heard as a priest.

My best mistake brought me peace of mind, fellowship, and a way
of life I did not think possible. One day at a time.

Best Mistake

Carol West
March 14, 2001

I was nine years old and home for the weekend from boarding school. My mother sent me off with my friends Smitty and Linda and two dollars to enjoy the local school fair in rural North Carolina. A five-minute walk from home brought us to the school field where we saw a variety of games, rides, and concession stands. Pizza was a big twenty-five cents a slice and pony rides cost the same.

I was fascinated by the sign that said "Fortune teller—have your palm read 25¢." We all felt the future was important. I was especially worried about boyfriends, since I was short and fat. Smitty looked average. Linda was a tall and graceful girl who guys just buzzed around.

We giggled at the sign and whispered for a few minutes. There were no customers, and I boldly said, "I'm going in." I opened the door and saw a lady wearing a bandana, long skirt, and shawl—a high school senior dressed as a gypsy. "Come in and sit down," she said. "Cross my palm with silver." A quarter did the trick. I sat down for what seemed like forever. The only thing I remember as she looked over my palm was that she told me I would: Have a long life, travel worldwide, and marry a man from a foreign land

After a two-minute reading, I was rushed out the door. The fortune teller now had a line of clients waiting. Smitty giggled when I came out, and Linda was suitably impressed. I wanted to go in again, but it was time to go home. I was happy, and I had a lot to think about. Fat Girl would marry someday. The gypsy told me so.

I moved to New York and became a reservation agent for a foreign airline and traveled worldwide. I married a man from England who I met in a pub on Third Avenue. Years later, he returned to London with my heart and our bank account. But at least I can always say that I was married.

My Best Mistake

John Cabello
April 9, 2003

Again this year I ask
Why? Why? Why?
Hasn't—in some ways—
My life been a mistake?

But this by no means
Tends as usual to
Help me understand
The human condition

It is obvious
That I do not have
Any real control, ruling
Their good perfect laws

So I keep on following
The rules, their rules
While I keep struggling
Fantastically to find love

Life in the best sense is being
Called father, dad, even daddy
Nonstop fathering until the last
Lapse of my own years.

I'm old now, but that was my best
On earth mistake, my own
Mistake that made me happy, so
Thankful you were born!

Lost Family

Paul Coleman
March 26, 1997

Jimmy passed away two years ago—
Hadn't kept in touch—
A common occurrence in our family
Yeah Jimmy, Uncle Jimmy.
The man was the essence of cool
Jazz musician vibes
Black velour broke down, sharkskin pants
Taught me the drums, gave me a hat
When I was eight years old.

Moms and Pops didn't dig him—
Too free, like a stylin' bird
Never married mother's sister, my
Aunt Betty, but they shared
A home over thirty years,
Shared a life many more.
Was a good man but wild
Totaled a Buick my aunt would
Buy him every year.
Nothing caged him
Throat cancer took him
Betty's got the ashes
Fellas still talk about him
Wish he was here.

The Hardest Loss

Janice English
April 18, 2001

The hardest thing I ever did was to take care of my son Shannon, who died in 1977. My son Shannon was born on St. Patrick's Day, March 17, 1971. He was my first child, and I still love him very much.

I consider myself a good mother and with no other knowledge to go by, gave him vaccines. I thought I was doing the right thing. He seemed to be growing normally. He was sitting up by six months, but he wouldn't crawl. I began to see that he couldn't hold himself up.

I took him to the hospital and they did a biopsy on him. They had me running around for a couple of days. I would always be looking for the doctor to find out what was wrong with him, but they were never around.

One day I got fed up and took him out of the hospital. Security tried to stop me, but I left anyway. However, before I left, a doctor told me he had something called Werning Hoffman's disease. There was nothing to be done. I was devastated and took him to another hospital, and they told me the same thing— there was nothing they could do.

I took care of him the best I could. He eventually was in a wheelchair. One day I went to the library and did research on the disease, because I knew the doctors weren't telling me everything. What I found out was that Werning Hoffman's disease was a rare form of muscular dystrophy and that the children never live beyond the age of five years old.

Talk about the world crashing down. I thought I was going to pass out in the library. I went home. I never told anyone else about this for at least three years. I kept it to myself.

I was always with him. As I look back on those challenging years, I realize the masks I had to wear. Inside I was dying as I watched him in his wheelchair, seeing that he couldn't run and play like other children. It just about killed me. He used to catch pneumonia often. I had to stick a tube down his throat to keep his lungs clear. I had to do it as though everything was all right.

Shannon was a happy child. He sang. He had a cousin a year younger who also lived with us, who used to get to do the regular children things like throw things out the window, call on the phone, and dial the operator. Shannon was going to a school for the handicapped, something I regret now. He still needed his lungs cleared—they called it being "suctioned." The most important thing about him was that he was wise beyond his years. You could talk to him about life. He had so much sense that even the doctors used to say, "He can't walk, but he sure can talk."

I should say before I go on that I got pregnant when Shannon was five. He told me I was having a girl, his sister, and her name was Tia, and that he would always look out for her. Tia was born December 8, 1976. She was premature, weighing two pounds and two ounces. She couldn't breathe on her own, so she had to rely on oxygen.

For a month, she was in the hospital, fighting for her life. Shannon told me she would be okay, and he was going to always watch over her. One night, after I suctioned Shannon, he said, "Mommy, I'm going to ask God to help me because I'm tired of being suctioned." The next day, I sent him to school. When he returned they gave him to me in my arms. They said he was asleep, but I knew he was dead. He died on January 4, 1977.

He was buried three days later. After the funeral, I called the hospital to see how Tia was doing. I found out that the time I buried Shannon was the time Tia came off the oxygen and started breathing on her own.

So you see—God does work in mysterious ways. One thing I learned for sure is that the world doesn't stop for your pain. You have to learn to go on and deal with certain things by yourself.

Lost Family

Carol West
April 23, 1999

My parents abdicated their responsibility for me upon their divorce, before I was two years old. I never heard from my father until I was eleven, except for a check for thirty dollars sent to my mother the first of the month, for which he got control of my religion.

My mother, in the midst of her over-medication, hypochondria, obsession, and ego, hysterically acknowledged me when it was convenient for her. I was left in the care of an unwilling grandmother.

At nine years old, I was packed off to a strict Catholic boarding school where I did not measure up or fit in. Dad approved and kicked in another fifteen dollars a month. They sent me to hell.

I developed a compulsive addictive personality, set adrift in a mad sea on a raft of concerned indifference. My parents showed up with their parents for support and protection from each other at my graduation and wedding. A "Do as I say, not as I do" attitude prevailed from my parents, who should not have been parents.

At fourteen, I prayed out loud, "GOD GRANT I NEVER HAVE CHILDREN," and he heard my request. My mom and her mom were shocked. Every woman wanted children, right? I once went to an astrologer who cast my horoscope by computer. She got my "House of Family," and her first question was, "Where are your parents? They don't appear anywhere on your chart."

Lost Family

Joe Negrelli
April 23, 2003

My family and I, who had marginal contact at best, went astray thirty plus years ago. I went into seclusion for ten years. I initiated contact after this ill-fated fallout. Slow going at first, but understandable since there were problems of pride, ego, and self-righteous indignation on all parties involved.

Fast-forward twenty years. Again I made a serious attempt to reconcile and got through. After I made a monumental effort with my sister, including a face-to-face meeting (her husband in tow), we had a grand time. After several meetings, she informed me that I had two half-brothers. She was a little vague about details and exact locations of these brothers. But she did provide me with enough information to initiate a search.

After several trips to the library to use the Internet and verify information, I called one of these men and asked his parents' names. So began the find of a lifetime. He contacted his brother and told him of my existence. The older one had little interest in finding out he had a brother, but the younger one was eager to connect with me.

I am glad that I put out a desire to know my brothers. I am extremely glad to know where they are. At first I was afraid to contact either one, then afraid of what to say. But it worked out and was cool in the overall.

Lost Family

Pierce McLoughlin
April 12, 2000

I grew up in a straightlaced Catholic community in New York in the fifties. I attended private Catholic school, where Dominican nuns wore habits. We went to children's mass on Sundays at 9:00 a.m. If we were not there we had to bring a note from our parents explaining our absence. School was regimented, with an emphasis on grades. Beware the principal's office. As Bill Cosby might say, "We never saw the belt but heard about it."

At home, there was more study and little television. My mother was the driving force with me, my sister, and brother. My dad meant well but could not bring himself to respect education or my mother's standard for scholarship. His idea of life was to work hard but play hard. Anything else was not terribly important.

My parents lived two separate lives in two separate bedrooms for almost twenty years. My mom's death from cancer ended our world of scholarship and genuine love, our Shangri-la.

New York would be a nightmare for me only for my mom's efforts to get me fairly educated. Although not a scholar, I developed a love for reading, poetry, and good thinking. I was very much taken by the mention of a Trappist monk who wrote of contemplative prayer. As a convert of Catholicism I never lost that identification with street people and their day-to-day problems.

After a suicide attempt, I finally put my life together. Learning of Alcoholics Anonymous and their philosophy changed me completely. I was no longer bent on chasing money or power. Doing twelve-step work I am like a therapist reaching out to others. I enjoy it and it brings me peace.

Thirst

Norman Clayton
March 31, 2004

I

I dream of love,
Always love
Always thirsting for old love,
A flood of love
I thirst for love,
Your old love flooding
Always light and love.

II

Hiccup the demons,
Swear by their dark light
We drank, father,
But only I showed
the terror, only I shared
the pain. Yet we loved
Each other.

In My Other Life

Carol West
March 7, 2001

In my other life, I can write eloquently, and people read me. I never have writer's block, and editors call me. I am able to pick topics that sell. I don't procrastinate. The work is handed in on time by deadline and published with few, if any, rewrites.

In my other life, I'm fascinating and fun, literally a literary party person. Other life, please come forth now.

In My Other Life

Janice English
March 7, 2001

In my other life I was royalty. I was a queen, and my husband the king was a very wise man although I didn't realize it at the time. I thought he was dull and boring, not much fun. I seemed to be much younger than him, and he spoiled me. I had everything I needed. I spent my days reading, delving into occult studies. I loved to read Tarot cards and I loved astrology. I enjoyed music and singing. I was very creative. I loved art, studied aromatherapy, and learned the right use of oils.

My husband had to rule the kingdom and make difficult decisions that affected many people's lives. He took his position seriously and was always concerned about acts of betrayal on his life or mine. He was a very structured person while I couldn't care less about structure.

There was a certain knight in the castle that I was attracted to. He was attracted to me. We succumbed to our passions. I called it fun. Out of this fun a child was conceived. It could not have been my husband's, because we had not slept together for some time. I had put him out of my bed, because I thought he was dull and boring. He was hurt, but I could do nothing about how I felt.

When I told him about the child I was carrying, he was extremely hurt. But he forgave me, like the generous person he was. When he did this, it dawned on me what a wonderful person he really was. Feelings of love, respect, and admiration grew in my heart for this man—feelings I never knew existed inside of me.

Our life together became sacred. I had the child, a girl, and our love grew stronger until the day he died. On his deathbed I told him I would love him forever. One day we will meet again and I'll know that he is the one I knew in my other life.

In My Other Life

Donald Mackey
April 3, 1996

I had my fantasy home already, but I lost it when I became homeless. Or did I lose it before I became homeless? Could it be that I no longer have that home because it was just a fantasy? My family was real. But that home was structured on things I never had and wanted my family to have, rather than wanting those things just because they were good or right or within reason.

My next home will not be a fantasy. It will be fantastic. It will be real and completely new. The children will be the same ones. Maybe some of them will be new.

In My Other Life

Jay Stockman
March 14, 2001

In my other life I'm a historian. I see how parts of the city I live in have changed over the years. When I first saw the rail trestle by 10th Avenue from 34th to 14th Streets, I found out more about its origin.

In the early 1900s, everyday life in the West Chelsea part of Manhattan featured a busy waterfront. Railroads were used a lot more. They moved cargo to and from the busy waterfront. The business was a danger to much of the foot traffic near 10th Avenue. In the 1930s, a rail trestle was built called the High Line. It connected the 34th Street rail yards, the Post Office at 30th Street, and many businesses along the road's length. The High Line saw much use with the busy Westside waterfront until truck transport began to replace rail trips.

Now in 2001, we've hit a crossroads with the High Line. It could be extended so it reaches parking at Pier 40 and ends at 34th Street, where a planned stadium would be built. After parking at Pier 40, folks traveling by the High Line could get to the stadium. Or, as some want, the High Line would be torn down, never to be used again.

The High Line grew less busy after the 1950s as pier traffic lessened. It has become almost abandoned through lack of use. A federal program relating to inactive railways caused growth of local groups wanting to resurrect what was once there. One of these groups in Chelsea is called "Friends of the High Line." When I first moved to Chelsea in 1974, I had no idea it would become such a hot, chic, commercial neighborhood. I want to push for the continuation of the High Line, finding a new life for this long, unused road.

The Other Me

Paul Coleman
March 19, 1997

Was once behind me
Irritating
Nagging
Bending my ear

(the other me)

Was once beside me
Leading
Pulling me towards
Unknown directions

(the other me)

I've succumbed to
Listened and was moved
Should have walked away
Now walks the streets
Sleeps on iron horses
Wakes to untold losses

I, The Mad Hatted

Carol West
March 10, 2004

I have developed a large collection of hats in the last two years. Catherine, the French patron saint of hat-makers and hats, chose to shower me with hats and a rack to keep them on. It began with a stylish summer straw on sale at Conway's for $1.99 plus tax. The chapeau gave me presence. I told people I was a hat person and the hunt was on.

I started to be given fabric hats, baseball caps, hats people were throwing out, new or maybe worn-once hats, hats with logos to wear while volunteering. At flea markets, wearing my toppers, I was given a lot of good used hats.

A friend died last July and the family, while dumping her belongings including her hats from the '40s and '50s, ran into me. I got two hatboxes with a mink hat, a rain hat, and two fedoras. My best friend went to Vegas and must have been held prisoner in some outlet store; she returned with two great hats for me, a pink suede bucket hat and a black flapping leather hat to hide my face under. In February on President's Day at another outlet on Long Island she found four more. "You now have hats for spring." Someone in my building was moving and said, "I have a stand for your hats." I don't ask. People see me in hats now and just hand them over.

People give me a second look, smile, stop to talk, and I have had my photo taken. Jim from church was running a summer street fair. I ran into him with my new beautiful straw with full-blown red rose. We took a photo, both hatted and smiling. I look like the Queen Mother. Just this week I got a straw cowboy hat at Jack's for 99¢.

I go home sometimes just to change hats, and with it attitude.

Hats

Norman Clayton
April 19, 2000

Salvation Army call to me, you must have a hat I didn't see.
Salvation Army hear my plea. I march and march and march.
Some more taking cans to the grocery store
Because I need some fine-feathered haberdashery.
Blue or pink or red or green
Then I wouldn't be a bum unseen.

Clothes

Paul Coleman
April 9, 1997

Seems so long ago
I know it wasn't yesterday
I wore my mohair black pants
And black suede shoes.

A funky ballroom, Smoky singing
"Lum de lum de li ah"
Mrs. Brown's daughter by my side
The Mashed Potato, the Twist
Claudine looking fly
In her tight skirt and white blouse
Filled to the brim.

Oh we were perfect
Perfect in every way
On the dance floor
On the street.

Life was good and time stood still
Had to be back by twelve midnight,
A little kiss, a belly rub, innocent
And slowly strutting home,
Head cocked high
In my mohair pants
And black suede shoes.

Fixing the Sole

Jay Stockman
March 15, 1995

Shoes and Jay start with several conditions. First, I need a certain type of shoe due to an injury affecting my feet. The right shoes have to accommodate my braces. The government pays for new shoes. Medicare shoes are cheap, thirty-five dollars a pair. I pay for repairs. Since I need shoe repairs twice a week, I have to find a shoe shop that 1) is close by where I live, 2) is skilled, and 3) can do the work at a cost I can afford, which is key.

One day coming from the shoe shop I stopped at a hardware store. I bought glue promising to be all I wanted this glue to be. Taking it home, I saw there were plastic containers in my kitchen that I took and cut up. The glue plus the plastic plus thumbtacks to hold things together while the glue dried were used to fix my shoes. That worked for a while.

Now I get Rockport shoes, which are more expensive. One pair lasts me two years. That's partly because when I use my wheelchair, I don't wear out my shoes as much.

Shoes

Bill Acheson
March 12, 1999

It was a January morning, and a wet, heavy snow was falling. I could not stay indoors as I had business to do that day. I left with a proper amount of clothing and a recently purchased pair of shoes.

These shoes were comfortable, which was a blessing. I looked down at them, and I was proud of them for their appearance and their fit. Fit is very important to me, since my podiatrist said my aching feet are due to foot bones shifting with old age.

The snow kept coming down and then the snow turned to rain. Slush was everywhere—big puddles formed at city intersections. Cars and cabs were splashing dirty water about. I walked about the city, low in cash, going from place to place. I started the day with a nice pair of shoes. At the end of the day, the shoes were soaking wet. It started when I had to step in a deep puddle at a corner. After this I did not care about my feet—I just marched on.

At home, I took the shoes off. They dried with that heavy salt stain all over them. I was disheartened. I let them stay under my bed for over a month. Finally, I got up the gumption to clean these shoes. I put them under the faucet and scrubbed them and let them dry. Then I used some saddle soap, finished the cleaning and polished the shoes.

Today there is a light snow outside and I am walking about the city again, enjoying the comfort of these same shoes. Yes, today is a better day.

Shoes

Nelson Blackman
March 29, 2000

A man drops a twenty-dollar bill on the ground unknowingly. Someone behind him picks it up and buys what he needs with it. Probably food or a cheap hotel for the night.

Someone throws away a pair of shoes that are in good condition, into the trash. A person who is unfortunately homeless without any good shoes at all may come along and use those shoes as a blessing.

That happened to me. I used to get off the PATH train at the World Trade Center, where I would see a well-dressed man of Caribbean descent. I was wearing a pair of raggedy sneakers that were five years old. One day he asked me, "What size shoes do you wear?" I said, "Size eleven." I have big feet. A few days later he saw me and handed me a pair of light brown work boots. "Here you are," is all he said. They weren't new, but they fit perfectly. Then he was gone. I thought he was an angel.

One man's trash is another man's treasure.

Part 2:

Stories, Secrets, and Dreams

Best Day

John Cabello
March 17, 2001 ,

"Do you know what is the best
Legacy of your dad?"
She answered him:
"Your big head, so big."

"Do you know what is bigger?"
He added, surprising her,
Knocking tenderly her chest
With his right fingertip.

"My breasts," she flamboyantly
Said in half fun, demanding
With other mimics the answer.
"Your heart and nobody else's."

Your dad's big head is only his
Indeed, we all laughed,
Enjoying sweet memories,
Days of togetherness.

My sweet daughter recalled
The incident, sealed with tears
As when they were toddlers
They are still deeply embraced.

Confronting the same realities
As adults now, I laughed
Sweet tears, flooded by my
Children, still my very own.

Great Day

Muhammad Siagha
March 17, 2004

Man becomes father
Woman becomes mother
Creation becomes being
Which in my eyes is an angel
Heaven on earth

Written in every language
Including sign language
And Braille for the world
To see, feel, hear, understand
Peace through poetry

I had a great day when I
Bumped into some friends
After eating lunch. We all
Sat down and shared
Our thoughts and ideas!

Opening Day

Carol West
April 9, 1999

I went to opening day in 1989 with my beau at the time, Joe. I called in sick to a job I hated, and went on Good Friday with a guilty heart. Because of the religious aspects and lying to my boss, I felt uneasy—but how many times would I get to this event?

Opening day at Yankee Stadium is a holy day. On the train on the way up, Joe traded our tickets for seats behind first base. It was a bright sunny day, and the batting instructor, Frank Howard, a player with my old Washington Senators, was hitting out balls to young players for warm-up. Wow.

The team looked great after a Florida winter. With Casey Stengel as part of Yankee history, I believed the Yankees would have a winning day and a winning year.

Joe, out to please me, grabbed a deflected fly ball that landed on the floor near us. He scrambled with half a dozen graying middle-aged men acting like six-year-olds to present the prize. Hot dogs, as only they can be at a ballpark, and sodas crowned the day. With an official program all was right with the world.

The Yankees didn't go to the playoffs that year. I got fired from my job a few weeks later. Last year Cardinal O'Connor spoke out against baseball on Good Friday in New York.

But that opening day was my day, and all was well.

It Was the Best Day

Peter Nkruma
March 17, 2004

It wasn't actually the best Best Day, but it was pretty good. I write a Web log on the Internet, and update it regularly at the public library. In it I ramble and rant on politics, celebrities, the lack of jobs in this economy, the pretty woman I met the night before.

I don't get paid for my Web log, I haven't yet figured out how to get advertising for it, and technically it's an eyesore. Electric blue and split-pea-soup green, my Web page is not sophisticated in design. But I love it: where else, aside from the Writers' Workshop, can I blather so freely?

Two weeks ago I wrote a parody of the evangelical Left Behind series on my Web page. I intended no harm, and people took it pretty well, judging from the e-mails. Only one person thought that I had blasphemed and promised to pray for my soul when it warmed the furnaces of Hades.

My parody on the Left Behind series was based on media celebrities. According to the Left Behind series, at the Rapture, God's Elect, one-third of the population will be whisked to Heaven, leaving behind their clothes, material possessions and, of course, those who have not yet seen Mel Gibson's *Passion*. With the best of intentions and malice towards none, I wrote on my Web page which media celebrities I thought were righteous, and who would be sentenced to life everlasting in a hot environment.

Since every writer secretly plays God, it was delicious fun to stand in judgment from a tiny Web page on a public library computer. I wrote that one of the most powerful editors of a liberal magazine, who has a reputation for not running articles by African Americans, would be Left Behind. It was therapeutic. I highly recommend the activity. But I didn't stop there. Madness overtook me. Old resentments and rejections by editors came tumbling forth from my electric blue and pea-green Web page.

One prominent glossy magazine writer, whom I always liked but who had a drinking problem, was whisked to heaven. I wrote, Godlike, "but he left behind a half full glass of Johnnie Walker Black whiskey—and he wants it back." I was hooked, going on and on, sending editors, writers, and TV hosts to heaven or the other place. When I was done, I logged off, feeling very satisfied.

The next day I went to the library to check my e-mail and found the mailbox full. That had never happened before. What was up? The responses were congratulatory, except for the Christian reporter from Georgia who prayed for my repentance. Apparently the editors of two important Web sites, Wonkette.com and Poynter.org, both "covered" my little parody. Political powerbrokers in the capital of the world's last superpower and journalists from around the country had read something that I had written.

One political columnist I'd mentioned wrote on his Web site that I was unjustified damning him to the Rapture. It was *so cool* getting that kind of attention. Of course, the next day, I was old news. But for one day, that best day, I was the talk of the town.

It Was the Best Day

Jeff Rubin
March 24, 2004

It was the best day when I found out I had made Performing Arts High School. *Fame*, that's right. "I'm Gonna Live Forever." Sung by Irene Cara. It was back on March 24, 1966, to be exact. I can still remember my guidance counselor bringing a monitor into my classroom and calling me down to her office. When I got to Ms. Gray's office, I had expected the worst. To my surprise she said I had been accepted. What a joyful day. But I've been getting ahead of myself. Let me jump back two months earlier to what I had to do. First off, this was the old Performing Arts High School located on 46th Street and Broadway, right in the heart of the Theater District. Its distinguished alumni include Al Pacino and Freddy Prinze, to name a few. So I was in good company.

I had to do two monologues and one improvisation. I remember going with Naomi Larkin and Heddy Steinburg. We couldn't find the building. It just so happened we ran into an old friend of mine named Dennis who was cruising Broadway hoping to hitch up in the navy. He led us to an old castle-like building. Very forbidding. We all went into separate rooms to do our auditions. My two monologues were *No Time for Sergeants* (a comedy) and *Winterset* by Maxwell Anderson (a tragedy) with the improvisations made up by the examiners. As luck would have it, I knew one of the students we had to pair up with. So I chose him, Tommy Epps. He had graduated two years earlier from Oliver Wendell Holmes Junior High School. I felt a little more relaxed. The first and second monologues went off without a hitch. Now came the improvisation. What the committee came up with was "I have been there before." Tommy Epps and I made out like we were in the joint. Let me add that one of the committee members was Bozo the Clown on TV. I actually kissed his nose, and I've never lived it down. Anyhow I was the only one accepted to Performing Arts in drama.

My Proudest Day

Donald Mackey
May 6, 1998

My proudest day in high school was when I decided to complete the last two years at evening school, so I could hold a full-time job during the day. It was a difficult decision after having spent the last ten years doing nothing but being a student. There were home chores and weekend tasks. But to suddenly change that routine was uncomfortable.

In fact, it was rather awkward, because I felt I was being taught the same subject matter over and over again. I was terribly bored. The night school students, mostly older adults, were boring also. Nevertheless, I was very proud of myself that I had the desire, courage, and patience to stay the course and graduate.

On Achieving Section 8 Housing

Norman Clayton
March 15, 2000

Three-thirty p.m. a balmy March first
Bring in pale squared sunlight against
My east wall.

My once ailing poinsettia is thriving.
It now seems more pink than red.
It is below the sunlight
Yet it glows like a cherry salesman
In my all white room.

Part of me says
It will at the very least
In a few months turn green
Like all the other plants.

But not the best part of me.
The best part of me
Wants it to keep its cheery glow.
March, it has been 29 years
Since my first breakdown

March, march march march
The world is good.

A Wild Ride

Donald Mackey
June 23, 1997

As I boarded the subway this morning, I accidentally bumped into a woman who was wearing an infant harness strapped in front of her. I humbly apologized. Then I noticed that she was carrying a teddy bear in the harness. It was dressed from head to toe in infant clothes. She worked her way to the other end of the car as if to get away from me.

I managed to squeeze in a narrow space on the seat between two men. The man to my left suffered from obesity. He took up three seats. The man on my right jabbed me in my side every time he turned his newspaper. I don't believe that either of those men wanted me to sit between them. But the new shoes I was wearing were not broken in and hurt my feet, so I needed to sit. As a subway passenger, it isn't easy to maintain a consistent train of thought. There are too many distractions.

A group of schoolchildren entered the car in their usual boisterous, giggling, playful manner. Two rabbis seated across the aisle were engaged in a conversation while a Hare Krishna troop stood over them. Several straphangers down, an African couple was dressed in traditional tribal costumes. All of us were looking down at the little battery-run toys that Japanese vendors were hawking on the train. Except the homeless man, stretched out sleeping on one of the seats, oblivious to everything.

Knowing that I would soon be getting off, I left my seat early to make my way through the crowd, past bicycles, babies in carriages, picnic coolers, and pets in cages. The door opened and I walked quickly out of the train into more of the same.

A Wild Ride

Peter Nkruma
April 23, 2003

By the time I was twenty, my attraction to Christianity was fading. Skepticism about the world was creeping in to fill the void. Then, by chance, I found meditation by way of a turn-of-the-century journalist named Peter Ouspenskii. He wrote an intimidating book, *In Search of the Miraculous*, chronicling his spiritual quest. It describes curious methods of meditation that increased memory and emotional attachments. It seemed eccentric, but contained the flavor of truth and a hint of danger.

The aim was to remember your passage through time as fully as possible as it was happening The longer one practiced remembering oneself, the impressions deepened and you inched toward a greater depth of perception.

When I started meditating, I kept forgetting to remember myself. Each time I initiated remembrance, seconds later I had wandered into forgetfulness. Only when I was back in my aim of remembrance I saw that I had lost concentration. Ouspenskii stressed the difficulty of remembering oneself. Sometimes it felt like all the forces of nature were allied against self-memory. Yet ironically, the longer one remembered oneself, the less threatening all outside forces became.

A Wild Ride

Carol West
April 13, 1997

The Poetry Project's memorial tribute to Allen Ginsberg was fabulous, like getting two oversized slices of your favorite cake and eating it all up. It included people who loved him, young friends gone gray, colleagues, neighbors, writers he'd encouraged, as well as composers. He apparently loved to sing and couldn't, but he gave a lot of enthusiasm in music. It was supposed to be from 12 to 4 p.m. at St. Mark's Church, but it started late and went well past four.

From where I was in the back I could see wonderfully but missed names and nervous comments. Many young people came. When certain old names were mentioned I heard people mutter, "Oh, he's here," and "Wow, he came." It was a packed house, standing room only. It was all photographed, recorded, and taped. There was silence of respect, to hear every moment, grab every crumb.

Patti Smith played "I'm So Lonesome I Could Die." Lou Reed read a poem. Armand Schwerner read Ginsberg. The moderator said some people were contacted and did not answer or show up. Maybe they couldn't wear their grief in public so soon.

His last young companion spoke of him in a loving old folk song and mentioned their last intimate meal together—a special rice, low-fat yogurt and a Diet Coke. The companion played a tape of Ginsberg chanting a new poem called "Gone Gone Gone." Gregory Corso, a wild man, was clean and sane in a moment of grief and promise unharvested. It was a '60s gathering where the past was made new again.

Ann Douglas spoke of going with Ginsberg to Jack Kerouac's funeral, where he told her, "Go up and touch Jack's face, so you'll know he's dead." Apparently, Ginsberg, in the Tibetan Buddhist tradition, did not wish to be touched after he died. She read from an advance copy of *Letters of Jack Kerouac, Volume II* where Kerouac writes of Ginsberg's encouragement, support, and love.

Peter Orlovsky had long gray hair, and wore a suit, clean-shaven, dressed to remember. He noted Allen would say, "Don't be angry, write a lot, as skillfully as you can." A longtime writer friend talked about his death and going out to cut up an old, large, fallen tree. He'd work an hour or so and kept saying, "I must call Allen and tell him Allen Ginsberg is dead."

My Hidden Talent

Bill Acheson
April 25, 2001

A talent is not a skill. Skills must be learned with practice, and often are not all that enjoyable. Talents are activities, skills that are easily mastered and excelled in. Often people do not burn out by excessive use of talent. Joe DiMaggio was a talented baseball player. I am a somewhat "has-been" skilled baseball player.

In career counseling, it was pointed out that I am skilled. I have a wide range of interests. However, I do not have that "staying power," the perseverance to make a career with progressive responsibilities out of any of my ventures. I burned out, pursued greener pastures elsewhere, moved or developed a nonlinear career path.

So what was lacking? What was hidden? Half joking, the career counselor said my career choices should have been more limited. It would be easier if I was less talented, less educated, less intelligent. That, along with being less creative, might have kept me in a structured job definition longer.

Though I have a wide range of talents, skills, experiences, and job titles, I have not had a passion for work. I lacked a stable anchor over time, a stable focus where I could build on past skills and experiences. I'm talking like a specialist, a technician. I was trained that way.

My father, daughter, and I are all college graduates in engineering. So what is that hidden talent that I am chasing? A successful, progressively responsible linear career like my father had? Too late for me—I went a different direction. Learning to enjoy where I've been, an interesting pilgrimage? Definitely a possibility, but I have problems with finding joy and gratitude in my past. If this is a talent, it's hidden.

Trying to find that elusive element that rearranges my past from a collage into an orderly, neat photograph. Still trying, maybe unrealistically. Can I unscramble an order of scrambled eggs? Or maybe accept it? Hard to do for a fixer, a problem-solver. I keep meeting that block, that puzzle, that entanglement that tells me to quit and move on. Finding meaning in life is a hidden talent that still eludes me. Someone said, "Life is a mystery to be enjoyed—not a problem to be solved." That is good for you; let me struggle on.

My Hidden Talent

Carol West
April 30, 1999

If I had to do it all over again, I'd pay more attention to my education and learning. I would have listened to my freshman algebra teacher Mr. Church's advice and gone to college. I wouldn't have let things bother me so much, obsessing over them for decades.

I would have taken the job offered at Goldwater in '64 headquarters and met Rich. I'd have listened to my inner voice and taken opportunities, living in Portugal for six months or indefinitely in Greece. I'd have drunk my way through France.

I'd have never gotten married, or then I'd have listened to my grandmother, who a month before my wedding tried to tell me I didn't have to wed. Barring that, upon returning from the honeymoon, I'd have gotten a divorce and run like hell to California.

I'd have lived life more fully, saved money, flown first class more often, taken more chances. I'd have listened more, talked less, and loved more greatly.

I'd have written about my life in a notebook and become a writer sooner. I never knew my writing was my magic.

My Hidden Talent

Jeff Rubin
April 18, 2001

My hidden talent began on my travels to a city in northern Spain off the coast of the Bay of Biscay called San Sebastian. Its original Basque name was Denostia. It is one of the most beautiful cities in all of Spain if not Europe. They say if Brigitte Bardot could create a city, it would be San Sebastian, with its amazing beaches and mountains.

Enthralled by the Spanish aroma of the city with its cooking, bull fights, and of course, the Spanish masters such as El Greco, Velasquez, and Picasso, I took my pencil and pad by the beach and began to draw. I wanted to capture the beautiful people and the church on the mountain.

While sketching the people, I had a sense that these beautiful people tanning themselves in the Spanish sun would be no more, which made me a little sad. So I had to draw them before they'd be gone.

Passers-by watched me while I sketched and said, "You are another Picasso! You draw very well." I thanked them and admitted that I'd never taken a lesson. My aunt saw my work and said I had talent and should go to Paris. To Paris! Just recently, an art teacher began to give lessons at the temple where I am a client. There, a woman named Laura recommended the class. Laura loved my sketches of Spain and showed them to the art teacher. The art teacher asked me to do a still life. I said I live in a black-and-white world. She said she would teach me color, which she did.

My Hidden Talent

Peter Nkruma
May 17, 2004

I never thought I was funny. I still don't. But I publish a Web log, where I react to current events and pop culture in an ironic voice. I have to, otherwise the enormity of my anger over my lack of work and money would make it unreadable. The fact that I play to an unseen audience balances out my enraged rhetoric.

In college I majored in philosophy and concentrated on Kierkegaard, the Greeks, and Shakespeare's tragedies. None of that is inherently amusing. My mother says I was a serious boy. I resigned myself to being a "serious" person, not the guy to go for levity.

My Web log changed that perception. After six months, the over-whelming reaction has been that I make people laugh. A writer for an alternative weekly in New York actually called me a "witty blogger." Who knew?

At thirty years old, I have never been referred to as entertaining, comical, funny, or witty. I saw myself as the overly studious type, reading a lot of Jewish intellectuals and debating issues in *The New York Review of Books* and *Dissent*, a leftist Martin Buber or Hannah Arendt wanna-be.

Yet now, after three decades, I find that I give people a laugh. I can be a funny person when I try. What a marvelous thing to discover. But I keep it to myself, since I have a reputation and gravitas to maintain.

Daughter of a Psychic

Thyatira English
April 24, 2002

It's hard sometimes when your mother has the gift because everyone thinks you do too. Everyone says that they don't believe. Then they will still ask if my mother could tell them anything. This is stupid, because if they don't believe in the first place, why bother asking? When she tells them something, they're not going to believe her anyway.

Friends of my mother rub on my sister and me, hugging us and buying us little gifts. I guess this is so they can get luck from us. What is it like to be the daughter of a psychic? You have the gift too but don't want to use it because you don't want to get used.

My Hidden Talent

Walter L. Schubert
April 30, 2003

Growing up I had to speak German at home—my father was very strict about it. I had to practice violin for one hour a day, one and one-half hours on weekend days. I had to be in by five, and I was always the last kid on the block to get in on the latest fads. It was right after World War II, and you can just guess who "the enemy" was when they invited me to play war. I had one friend in the neighborhood who was like me because he had to speak French at home. He, too, was never invited to play baseball, and in his case he turned to art rather than to music as I did.

When I was twelve my sister, mother, and I went to Germany by boat—something not as luxurious as it is today. The result was that I had to stop playing the violin. Within a few weeks, my fluency in German greatly increased. I learned to play with other children. So when we returned after two months, I held it over my parents that their own skills in German were lacking. I was not able to pick up the violin after my long absence and neglect. Never again was I called "Wally." From then on it was Walter.

I had a friend with whom I developed a fascination for technical things. We went to explore the Museum of Natural History. My sister introduced me to chamber music of the Baroque period. This reawakened my appreciation for the violin, and I realized that I had a gift I did not fully appreciate. While I let my language skills languish, my musical skills grew.

I neglected my language skills until I started my ten-year stint of graduate study in Chicago. While holding on to my music, I regained my language skills by singing in ethnic choruses. I was active as a violinist/violist in orchestra and chamber music while I remained in touch with my friends who were full-time students.

Toward the end of my stay in Chicago I was asked if my parents were well educated. I said no. But I think that, while I was a child, those glasses of mine did more than help me see better. They prompted others to guess that I was the bright kid in the class.

My Hidden Talent

Jay Stockman
April 18, 2001

I had a near-fatal injury from a car accident when I was seventeen. My friend was driving a 1963 Pontiac Tempest, not such a well-built car. I was a passenger in the right front seat, the suicide seat. The car skidded 150 feet, into a telephone pole. I hit the roof. Physical damage was not immediately obvious. What damage there was became noticeable once I tried to move. I could not walk for six months. Forty years later I still see a physical therapist.

Initially I was mad. But I went to college shortly after my injury. I studied Special Education. In school and from my own life, I saw the great effect productive work had on me and others doing physical rehab.

I found out about the Holy Apostles Soup Kitchen in a local newspaper story. I began doing regular cleaning work at the church in 1989. The effects of my cleaning work weren't immediately obvious either. But if I missed several days of swabbing the walls, I was told the effect was noticed.

My Special Education training, combined with my personal experience, told me this soup kitchen was a good place to work. I could see the useful effect of what I did, both physically and emotionally. Here I used my hidden talent. Real or not, it made me feel good.

Wish List

Nelson Blackman
May 13, 1998

If I suddenly became rich, I would buy myself a new pair of black leather loafers and red and white Reebok sneakers. I'd get a Rolex watch with Roman numerals, a dark blue Lamborghini car, and fancy Italian suits, like the kind in *GQ* magazine. Then I would go to Europe or Israel or the Caribbean. I always wanted to go St. Croix and St. Thomas, where I would hang out on the beach drinking tequila. Then I'd give the rest of my money to charity, which is a better blessing. I would remember to feed the homeless.

Wish List

Peter Nkruma
May 7, 1999

If I had a million dollars, I'd pack a bag and head off to the airport to acquire a ticket to the most remote island off the coast of Greece. I'd ask the travel agent which islands are undergoing civil war, or had State Department advisories. Whichever place she'd mention in hushed tones would be my destination.

Right now the dollar is strong everywhere, and I'd imagine it would be very strong on a rustic Mediterranean island. I'd take up fishing in a fishing village, gain the natives' trust, drink Ouzo in the scorching summer heat, stalk octopi in the dark sapphire seas, and give charitably to anyone in need. At night, I'd involve myself in whatever conceivable intrigue the Mediterranean offered. I'd want to live dangerously.

When I was sure that the minerals of the jagged coast had penetrated my bloodstream—I would buy a farm on the rockiest, most ungovernable soil. Then I would stock the farmhouse with books on Greek philosophy and poetry and spend my nights basking in the afterglow of a campfire surrounded by the dying scents of roasted goat and feta cheese—singing Ionian hymns to pagan gods.

I would guide my sheep across the rugged country, muttering commands in Greek, aided by an old sheepdog. I would find startling mountain views to rest by. I would also farm olives, haggle with the village women, and hunt wild boar with the men. At night, when I was alone and all the animals were asleep, I'd sit under the dazzling stars and break out a book on ancient Greek geometry, put a good tape in the stereo next to me, and read. I would marry a young village woman to share this stark and simple beauty. Once my money was exhausted, I would remain a shepherd-farmer-philosopher on my remote island forever.

My Wish List

Jay Stockman
May 1, 2002

If I put "realistic" in front of "wish list" I flash to motorized wheelchair. Though many community adjustments (like commonly found curb cuts, accessible buses) are already in place, they were not matched in advancements by my power wheelchair. Unfortunately this chair seems to be meant for exclusive indoor use and more than a little outdoor travel caused breakage. I got the chair in the first place because of hardships I had getting around the city.

When my friend Arthur passed away, I inherited his manual wheelchair. It is slower and flimsy, and it pulls to one side. On the other hand, it's making my arm muscles stronger. Also it's good that for ten dollars a year, I can swim at the pool across the street at the Chelsea Recreation Center.

Waiting for my bulky power chair to be fixed, I wish for full mobility for the disabled. Most people think of disability as a short-term affair—they do rehab, get better, and leave able-bodied. For me it's a long-term deal. Maybe I'm experiencing these problems so I can be a pioneer in this field. I wish this is true, but I don't really think it is.

My Team

John Cabello
April 7, 2004

The Knicks were it, since the beginning
Of the nineteen-nineties. All of them were
So young, so alive, real wonders. Especially
When season-by-season they grew stronger.
Allan Houston, Latrell Sprewell and two
Smaller, faithful guys who were sold
And recalled when the illusion went off
When they were so close to being champions
Of the east and west coast. I think it was twice
David Robinson's faith was stronger. Plus he
Was also the tallest of all, from his Texas spurs,
His rings champion winning. Sports was never
My own, due to my religious Sundays,
I had to postpone. Real life took its way
To deprive me of sports and entertainment.
Anyway I was always happy having to work
Nights and Sundays so I could speak by telephone
To my family, sharing my children's joys at the end
Of the other world, which was even better than
If I could afford to buy tickets to the Knicks game.

My Team

Carol West
April 7, 2004

I don't have one, never did.
No one, not even a hungry dog,
Would follow me down the street.
I am a team unto myself.
I am a team of one.

Gamblers Anonymous

Norman Clayton
April 7, 2004

My team
Is anonymous
My God
Seems anonymous.
Sometimes—often
He is with my
Anonymous brothers
And often I
Am with them—
And with him.
But not always
Which is when
I need them both.

My Team

Joe Negrelli
April 7, 2004

Boy, I rarely feel that I have a team at all, but I know that there is a parliament out helping me. People, friends, and strangers who pray for me. The Friday Church van and my friends at Holy Apostles who have been so kind as to mention me in prayer. Strangers who may have learned of me or someone else from a friend at Holy Apostles who prays daily. People in the universe who pray to God frequently. Thank you all for your kind thoughts and generous consideration.

My Team

Jay Stockman
April 7, 2004

At the Soup Kitchen the team of folks I work with is mostly men, rarely women. Three to six of us work at the tray table from 9:30 to 12:45. How the team of tray handlers is made up is modified by variables. One can be the number of trays we handle, which changes with the time of the month. The Soup Kitchen sees more folks toward the end of the month, when guests' resources (welfare checks, loose money, food stamps) run dry.

On the receiving line, we take the trays as they're handed in. We separate silverware, stacking it so they pile neatly in the gray bins, and make sure they're carried inside (with spoons also). Taking filled garbage bags out and relining the plastic garbage cans are occasional necessities. Physical limitations, like mine, may keep some from doing certain functions. This is made up for by other folks working harder in other areas. My team works well in our short time span. Then we eat together.

If you volunteer, you can pick and choose which foods you want because of allergies or health reasons. I'm allergic to egg yolk and don't eat meat. It feels better to eat with the volunteers, after we've built up hunger and felt like we were helping.

A Food I Cannot Eat Anymore

John Cabello
April 21, 2004

My strong sister Amelia is allergic
To many foods except for crabs
Of the South Pacific. She is exactly
My opposite. I am not allergic to
Anything except for those crabs that
Forty years ago made me close to death.

A Food I Cannot Get Anymore

Joe Negrelli
April 21, 2004

I can't get Italian rolls.

Years ago when I was young, I remember in Greenwich Village, there was a real Italian bakery on Carmine Street which was owned and operated by real Italians (with accents, and born and raised in the old country).

Each morning as I walked down the street, I could smell the bread and other bakery goods from at least two blocks before the shop. Heaven must smell like that. Sweet homemade bread, rolls, and other Italian specialties wafted through the streets of downtown New York, calling all residents, friends, and neighbors to the shop.

I wish I could remember the name of the owners who might have opened another bakery elsewhere. Maybe they went back to Italy.

Hot Food

Jay Stockman
March 1, 1995

Chelsea's a great place. It's the home of the Communist Party U.S.A., as well as the General Theological Seminary for the Episcopal Church. The soup kitchen for hungry people complements the City Housing Authority developments that have homes for people who may otherwise be homeless. What's the soup kitchen got that's so great? It has what its name says. Hot food. Served in a nutritious, balanced way. The food looks and tastes good. There are no obligations that come with it either.

Food

Norman Clayton
May 9, 2004

My favorite food is thought. I think about thought
All the time these days, hungry even before breakfast.
Thought sandwiches, the soul food. Just me and Hamlet
But he didn't really live. Sweet thoughts are nutritious
But devilled eggs and devil's food cake is absolutely taboo.
Too much stale bread isn't good for you. Eat that thought!

A Gentile Is Passed Over on Passover

Carol West

Well, it's that time of year again, and I was not the chosen one. Passover has passed for the twentieth time, and I still haven't been invited to a seder.

I moved to New York in 1967 from the South, and my first several years here were a cultural adjustment and a food delight. My only previous experience with Jewish food was a Hebrew National hot dog. I was overwhelmed by knishes on the street, horseradish, lox, good bialys, seltzer water, and chopped liver. My landlady, Mrs. Gruenberg, cooked me chicken soup with matzo balls when I was sick, but I preferred her kreplach. Rugalch became my pastry of choice.

When Passover came it was matzo sandwiches with cream cheese and jelly for me. At my office, feasts from the night before were discussed and recipes were exchanged. Goodies in abundance were brought from home with the explanation, "Bubbe made too much." I ate dense chocolate Passover cakes, macaroons—plain and chocolate—special chicken and a memorable apple-nut dessert.

How could I get myself invited to this yearly festival, I wondered. I gave myself a year, then another. It became an obsession, like the prom.

With so many Jewish friends, associates, and lovers, I became Don Quixote, searching for an invitation to the elusive holiday meal. Each year, I made efforts to secure a coveted seat. I gently asked, "Are you preparing anything special?" and "How long does your seder last?" Finally, I was blatant and asked, "Will you be having any guests for dinner this year? I could be enticed over." My friend Stella said, "We always go to a hotel for Passover." My friend Mitch said, "We're going to my mother-in-law's." My landlady told me, "My dream has come true. I'm spending Passover in Israel." Another colleague said, "It's my friend's turn." Agnes, a recent convert, told me, "My husband wouldn't understand." You figure that one out. Doesn't anyone believe in the kindness of an invitation?

In 1985, I worked with a young German named Helmut. He wasn't here a month when he got his invitation for the first-night seder. His only comment was "nice meal." I'm still at square one.

I am prepared to be a superstar guest. I located a strictly kosher candy store on Madison Avenue, so I'd take the right chocolates. I have a connection who has a connection in Brooklyn, so I can get a box of fresh matzo for twenty dollars a pound. Money is no object. Of course, I'll send a thank-you note with a basket of fresh fruit the next morning to my host and hostess.

If I am ever invited, I'll accept in a minute, even for the eighth night dinner. Perhaps after several years of good behavior, I can work my way up to the second night. And then maybe even a cherished seat at first-night Seder.

This year I'm starting a new organization: Invite a Gentile to Your Passover Seder. Maybe guilt is the way to go.

Published in *The Forward*, April 17, 1998

That Cheeky American Wine

Carol West

When I moved to New York City in 1967, I was in lust and living with Robin, a British wine snob who had no money but did have standards. On a small budget, he bought acceptable French wines. Spanish wines were for summer sangria, Italian wines were used in a pinch, and American wines were a joke to him.

Being a southerner from Virginia, and the child of a "dry" household, I had much to learn. I saw how serious this subject was to Robin when his cousin Jack arrived for our first Thanksgiving dinner together, bringing with him two bottles of white Burgundy.

So I developed a special relationship with Sid, my wine man at the local liquor store. He oversaw and encouraged my selective wine purchases. One Saturday night I arrived at Sid's with a deluxe steak, desiring a complementary grape. He suggested a California wine called Cabernet Sauvignon. I was silent. It did come from a vineyard with a French name, Beaulieu, and had a cork with foil and a label dated 1969. But at three dollars a bottle, which was a lot for a bottle of American wine in 1971, I wasn't so sure. Sid said he'd tasted it, and it was really good. Finally convinced, I bought it.

At home my steak was praised, and I'd made the perfect salad. But Robin said the wine was "unacceptable." He said, "How could you spend money on this?" He dismissed the unopened bottle to the side and brought a German Riesling to the table. "Would you like me to go back to the wine store?" I asked. He ignored me. Over the following week, the bottle, put aside, was looked at as an error of my judgment. Sid asked, "Did you like the wine?" I said, "I'm saving it," but I was really just saving face.

Well, lo and behold, within a year *Time* had a cover story on California wines titled "There's Gold in Them Thar Grapes: A Brief

Guide to California Wine." American wines were finally becoming respectable. The top bottles of American wine were listed in the magazine and mine was there! I carefully placed the now holy item on a top shelf for a very special occasion and left the *Times* article for Robin to read, so he could see the error of his ways.

Robin and his snobby Continental friends supposed my wine might be drinkable. Sid proudly displayed the article in the store. My in-house wine expert began just pretending the wine didn't exist. I protected the bottle though two moves, our wedding and a tag sale. In 1978, we relocated to Florida, and one cold March afternoon we finally decided to drink the bottle. By this time California wines were fine and correct, and the prices were high.

I cooked a gourmet meal, and the bottle was opened. The cork smelled fine, and the wine was aerated for at least an hour. Two correct wine glasses were brought out, the wine was poured, and the reward was a beautiful bouquet. The sublime wine was well rounded, with a mellow magnificence in the mouth. The meal was forgotten. This was a bottle of wine to be fought over, and we did just that. I beat him out for more than half the bottle. After all, who had believed in and cherished this treasure all along? Robin agreed that the wine was wonderful, and said, "So, why didn't you buy two?"

Published in *Wine Spectator*, August 3, 1997

Only in New York

Pierce McLoughlin
April 11, 2001

Things that happen only here can be seen in the ordinariness of everyday life. In the daily lives of subway people opening and closing doors on a subway, the sanitation workers, a traffic guard. There are simple kindnesses that you find only here.

I remember helping a little kid across a street. His mother was on the child's left side. I was on the right. When the light turned to green, the youngster lifted both hands—one for Mom, the other hand for me. This may not sound like much, until you realize that I was a total stranger. I knew neither the parent nor the child.

The child, in simple fashion, grabbed his mom and me. After all, I was an adult. Wasn't I? All three of us crossed the street. The mother was a bit embarrassed but the child was not. We all three got across in fine spirits. Safely. Only in New York.

"Unless you become as little children, you cannot enter the Kingdom of God." Trust. One day at a time.

A True Story

Carol West
April 7, 2004

The homeless man was "on." Jumping up and down, bobbing, weaving, smiling, shouting, smelly, and sweating. "Please," he cried. "Give me a dollar. Pleeeease, I need a dollar," he said to everyone who walked by. He was adamant.

I don't know why, I stopped. Not that I had a dollar to give him but I asked, "Why do you want a dollar?" Still smiling and in my face, he shouted, "I need a dollar to get married."

I made a decision and gave him my change (not a dollar). "This is so you won't get married," I shouted as I walked away. "It will cost you too much to get single again."

He laughed as he collected a new dollar from the next passerby. No questions asked.

Melville and the F Train

Norman Clayton
March 17, 2004

Drowned names
Scratched by soon
Drowning sailors.
Yo Maria! Yo!
Your black roots
Still clutch your
Opened thighs, your
Scarred, etched and
Tortured thighs. Look!
Enter scarred me,
Tortured me, who finds
Black humor in the
Stained stainless steel,
The fluorescent light,
Shining now, at midnight,
Underneath the East River.

Only in New York

Nelson Blackman
March 10, 2004

While growing up in Harlem, not only did my parents take care of me, but also my neighbors. There was always a watchful eye. My mother had a good friend named Carol, a tall black lady. She and her husband Willis were also from the South. They owned the cleaners down the street where they worked, I think it was called Carol's Cleaners. If my mother had an appointment, she would leave me at Carol's and they would watch me until dinner. Carol was nice. She had a television set on the other side of the counter. She liked soap operas. We'd watch them half the day. I liked *All My Children*. Her favorite was *The Young and the Restless*. She'd give me potato chips and Coke. Then my mother would call and tell Carol to send me home for dinner.

My Secret Place

Carol West
April 14, 2004

These days, flying under the radar and not being noticed is just fine.

I asked a boyfriend not to go through my messy dresser drawers, and he took it to mean I thought he might steal from me. A massive argument and breakup then occurred.

I had a boss when I was a secretary in a factory who went through everyone's personal property on weekends (he had keys to everything), trying to live his life vicariously through our small possessions. I took everything home on a weekend except ... I hope he got a kick out of my sanitary supplies.

My secrets always had to be within. Nothing said, nothing done, nothing used against me.

My Secret Place

Norman Clayton
May 3, 2004

Yellow dandelions dot
The green green cemetery.
My ego prevented the truth

I struggle ridges
You've got your Cadillac
Climb my eagle's wings

Mirror mirror fall
Gave myself a golden head
Masquerading now

The Secret Hideaway

Joe Negrelli
April 14, 2004

When I was in junior high school, the family and I moved to our second apartment on Chapman Street.

We had a sizable closet in the main room which also acted as dining-living-family room. In any case, I would go into this walk-in size closet and sit with the door closed; just a line of light from the bottom of the door so I could see and hide.

Sometimes people would come home, and I would sit listening to what they had to say, if anything, about me, the house, or other complaints regarding the family. It was like I was invisible and could watch from afar.

How I long for another big closet to hide in.

Secret Place

Bill Acheson
March 26, 1999

We all need a time and a place where we could be our true selves, a personal shrine to retreat from the busy, innate clutter and pain of life. We need a quiet time to commune in safety, with that which is pure and peaceful, which transcends this world and uplifts our spirit.

For myself it is a time in the morning before leaving home and a time in the evening before sleeping. I have had periods in my life when I was able to keep the morning discipline of prayer, reading, and meditation. But all too often, the schedule and pressures of the upcoming day overwhelm these yearnings of the soul, and I start the day handicapped. Today is such a day.

But before I sleep, the evening discipline is much more firmly established. I must really be very tired and fall into sleepfulness to miss my prayers and scripture readings. I often can't sleep and feel "incomplete" without saying at least my prayers. Sleep seems better with God.

My Personal Shrine

Ronnie Eisen
March 26, 1999

Once, when I was a teenager, I was wandering in Prospect Park in Brooklyn. I came upon a strange little hut by the lake. I decided to sit there and gaze at the water. Then it occurred to me that the place was extremely filthy and littered with old leaves, beer cans, and cigarettes. I was suddenly seized with an overwhelming desire to make this place my personal shrine. That is exactly how I thought of it in my mind. It was no longer a dirty little hut in the middle of Prospect Park. It now assumed all the exaggerated proportions of an outdoor temple in Tibet, where hundreds of pilgrims came to pray and make offerings to Lhasa. To see the Dalai Lama.

I could smell the incense, see the prayer flags waving in the wind, hear the chanting. It was now almost a civic duty to take care of the hut and return it to the place of sanctity it had once been.

After that day, I never returned to the little hut in the park, but I will always remember vividly that little imagined hut.

My Secret Place

Jay Stockman
April 14, 2004

It's in the entryway at the Church of the Holy Apostles where, every Wednesday afternoon for ten or twelve weeks during the spring, the Writers' Workshop meets. That it's run by folks (writers and college teachers) who know their subject well is a plus. The cooperation we get from the Kitchen and the Church is good too.

The Workshop is characterized by the absence of put-on styles or pretentiousness. We share our feelings through what we write. Advantages center around diversity, warmth, and being together. The shortcomings relate to time and duration. I always hope for some continuation after the annual reading, which doesn't happen. I wish the Writers' Workshop lasted longer and continued year-round, like the Soup Kitchen. I miss it when it ends each year.

If I Hadn't Seen It, I Wouldn't Have Believed It

Donald Mackey
April 2, 1996

On a bright and sunny day when I was about eight years old, my father drove our family to the top of the Blue Ridge Mountains in Virginia for a picnic. He had borrowed a panel truck. He was at the wheel, and I was with my mother, brother, and two sisters seated on kitchen chairs in the back of the truck. There were two doors at the back, and the doors had small windows at the top of them.

On the way up the winding mountain I began to notice, especially as we were about halfway up the mountain, that there were no guard rails around the narrow winding road leading to the top of the mountains. There was no flat land area at any point between the foot and top of the mountain. There just appeared to be this massive rock center around which the narrow road, barely wide enough for two lanes, wound in a steeplechase. When we reached the top of the mountain, we had to walk close to the edge in order to see what appeared to be a miniature town below.

We began our trip back home. At about one-third of the way down the mountain, the brakes on the truck stopped working. The only words spoken were when my father said the brakes were not working! The kitchen chairs were sliding from side to side of the truck as my father frantically maneuvered the truck around the winding path, picking up momentum. All I could imagine was the truck bumping into the side of the mountain and bouncing or rolling out of control. I did not think about dying. I don't think that I understood it. I think I just thought we would all be severely injured. I remember feeling very sorry for my mother.

Then my father screamed that the brakes were working. From that moment we crept down that mountain at a snail's pace. Watching my father manipulate that truck seemed like a miracle to me even at eight years of age. If I had not seen it, I would not have believed it.

If I Hadn't Seen It, I Wouldn't Have Believed It

John Cabello
April 19, 2000

He was just a little baby, just about sixty minutes old. Sucking his mom's young nipple, and he heard me clearing my throat so congested by the emotions. Jim, my baby, my last baby boy.

Now he's six feet, four inches. But when I see him, love still comes to my chest. Just listen to my heart pump. With eyes just the way he used to be as a toddler. When he tells me, "Dad, I love you," that is all I need.

If I Hadn't Seen It, I Wouldn't Have Believed It

Clarence A. Clarke
April 2, 1996

If Mary Magdalene had not visited the tomb in the Garden that first Easter morning, she would not have been the first of Jesus's followers to witness the savior's resurrection from the grave and his all-powerful victory over death.

In different books of the Gospel, we read of the events leading up to the crucifixion of the humble Nazarene. He is despised and rejected, a man of sorrows, acquainted with grief, and we hid, as it were, our faces from him. He was despised and we esteemed him not. But he was wounded for our transgressions. He was bruised for our iniquities. The chastisement of his peace was upon him, and with his death we are healed.

Mary, the once-sinner of Magdala, moved, overwhelmed by the great compassion of the Master. The same Jesus, who cleansed those with leprosy, fed thousands, healed the lame and the deaf, was persecuted so vigorously and dramatically by what appeared to be the very people who had benefited from his ministry and spiritual healing. Mary was a privileged witness of the risen Lord, coming from the depths of a contrite heart.

If I Hadn't Seen Him

Peter Nkruma
April 30, 2003

I met Jerry Kim in Brattleboro, Vermont, a decade ago. Jerry was an Asian man who spoke in an even, almost monotonous tone, but said the most fascinating things. He was interested—no, strike that—obsessed with personality and his own eccentric theory of human psychology.

Jerry Kim was deeply secretive about himself, which only added to the fascination factor. The only personal information that he ever disclosed was that he went to very strict Catholic schools as a child in California and that he was resentful of his mother for making that decision. Nothing more. If I pressed him on revealing other details, he would nimbly deflect my interrogation.

Jerry Kim seemed to have digested every book imaginable: the Great Books, the Eastern Classics, the Apocrypha, pre-Socratic fragments, African myths and fables—everything. When he was happy, he would whistle portions of classical music. One time I asked him what was on his internal radio. He answered, "'The Queen of the Night' aria from Mozart's *Magic Flute*," as if that were obvious.

Not only had Jerry Kim seemingly digested the total of human knowledge but he exuded an air of certitude. To me, at nineteen, the idea of certitude of knowledge was fascinating. Back then, my day consisted of chasing women. Jerry would materialize and dematerialize in my life at the oddest moments. Looking back, I cannot see what Jerry got out of our friendship. He didn't drink, wasn't interested in chasing women, and was much more intelligent than I was. I guess he needed someone to talk to as much as I wanted to listen.

Jerry Kim always wore a jacket and tie, never shouted, walked slowly, and appeared at odd moments of the day, without calling up, as if people had nothing more important to do than to wait for him.

Jerry Kim also had a very dry sense of humor. One could almost miss it if he did not give away the joke by his sly smile. I was interested in vague and silly New Age notions, and I asked him if he could try a "past life regression" with the subject. "I could do that," he said dryly, "if I was corny." A smile played on his lips. He would say the same thing whenever I asked him for his astrological sign. He loathed astrology.

Any time I would suggest getting beers or going to a party was Jerry Kim's cue to exit. It was as if he was allergic to having a good time. Then, one day, Jerry Kim vanished, or rather, I moved to Maryland. Although Jerry is no longer a part of my life, pieces of conversation still come back to me and exert influence. Often I will read a book and Jerry's comments on the author's personality will enrich my experience. Jerry Kim is probably a very original and eccentric psychologist now, or a guru in the Mustang region of Nepal. He was, without a doubt, the strangest person I have ever met.

Like a Movie

Carol West
May 1, 2001

Even in the slow-motion rerun of my life, I never saw it coming.

As a victim of an off-the-wall, dysfunctional childhood, no one prepared me to grow and cope. A part of the scared child remains alive more than four decades later. I heard adults intone, "when you grow up," but some people don't grow, and never really cope with life.

No one prepared me for the good times in life. No one spoke about having success. No one told me to be more than a homemaker. No one told me to save money or you'd be poor. I was not advised to set goals and keep setting new ones. The saddest disappointment was learning to live without money, friends, family, and hope.

I never saw a life of poverty coming.

My Life Was Like a Movie

Jeff Rubin
April 25, 2001

My life was like a movie the day I went deep-sea fishing on the island of Madeira, a possession of Portugal. We were going after blue marlin, as in *The Old Man and the Sea* by Hemingway. So here was a Portuguese captain and his mate, a five-person English crew and one American. You can guess who was the American.

We went out early in the morning and the Madeira natives wished us luck. It was September, the waters of Madeira still warm enough to catch the blue marlin. I was shocked to see the blue marlin up this far north as I thought they spent all their time in the Gulf of Mexico or the Caribbean. I knew we would have to go now or they would make their run back to the Gulf. So here we were going after them. We used very heavy poles with giant reels, and onto each hook was a phony piece of squid. I said to myself, "What a dirty trick to lure him in."

Each pole was set onto sockets around the boat. We went trawling for what seemed like hours. We caught a giant fish. The Portuguese captain said he had seen him for days. The captain, with his binocks, aimed at the creature and proclaimed, "Yes, it's a blue marlin. And a big one—about four hundred kilos." That would make it about seven hundred pounds.

With that, the line buzzed from the reel, making a whirling sound. The line spun forward. The blue marlin breached up out of the sea—like a cat that had just been shocked. The English girl who was part of the crew began screaming and running away from her pole as it was the one that was hit. I was thinking, "What a coward. I thought English girls had backbones, stiff upper lips, and that rubbish. I guess not." Anyway, we had to let the fish run. Jerking the pole would cause the fish to get away.

Eventually we landed him and brought him back to shore. We had pictures taken and then took him to market to be sold—for Madeiran tourists' plates. I felt sad that the fish was lost. But I did get to keep the bloody sword—which is actually the jaw of the marlin—as a souvenir.

As In the Movies

John Cabello
April 25, 2001

As in the movies I am touching a dream.
Since a year ago when I first became involved
With writing. Since then every Wednesday
I am in the room, spiritually, really creating.
I also got the habit to write every day, just
One page a time. Or at least I got the habit
To try. Whatever may happen—either beauty,
Ugliness or many times something undefined,
I see all of us, sharing verbs, words, the real
Root of God's spirit in us, longing to make work
Of high value. I have seen us as celebrities,
A positive force built up massively until we are
Valued by society and culture. Let us meet next
Autumn at least at the park, in front of the building
When our book will be produced, as if to say
We are important, our lives a mystery that counts!

Like the Movies

Walter L. Schubert
April 2, 2003

Two celebrities I met during my years in Chicago were Wernher von
Braun and Werner Heisenberg. I call them "the two Werners." The
first was my boyhood hero, a practical man who was taken from his
native Germany as part of the war loot, much as the Romans hauled
off philosophers after defeating the Greeks. It was hoped by the
Americans that Wernher von Braun would become bored with the tin-
kering with captured V2s and might become depressed, turn to drugs,
and maybe—just maybe—even commit suicide.

It didn't work out that way. Wernher von Braun was a man who
understood the historical sense. He knew that the Space Race was
inevitable. It was just a matter of "when." All his time, effort, and
resources were consumed in his careful observations of the developments in Washington and the Soviet Union. And all this time he posi-
tioned himself accordingly. Then the first Sputnik was launched, and
America was caught by surprise and embarrassed. There was a knock
at the door. Enter Wernher von Braun. "Here I am, gentlemen. Can I
help you?"

I heard von Braun speak at the Steuben Society convention held
at the Germania Club in Chicago in 1970. It was a canned lecture,
and he may not have appeared to have been very charismatic. But he
made himself well understood, and one saw the lifetime of experience
written all over his face. Yet, there are those who, even today, question
if this man should not have been killed at the time he was captured.

The other Werner—Werner Heisenberg—gave a lecture to a general audience at the University of Chicago in 1974. Unlike Wernher
von Braun, who could still have swept the women off their feet, this
Werner Heisenberg impressed me as a kind, calm, and pleasant old

gentleman. He spoke of his two most notable discoveries—his Uncertainty Principle and matrix mechanics—and his doubts as to the viability of any current effort to unify the universe. His only exception to this doubt was the possibility of unification under US3 symmetry—but even here, he had serious reservations.

As I grow older I have renewed my appreciation for the life and work of Werner Heisenberg. I can see how closely allied was his perspective to that of Martin Heidegger, the German philosopher, who can teach us to live resolutely in the face of chaos.

As I grow older still I see the absurdity of this chaos and contemplate, in my loneliness, the cold dark and the empty desolation of the vast reaches of interstellar space. Anyone out there?

I Had My Fortune Told

Thyatira English
March 14, 2001

I have my fortune told about every month. I like to have it done. It's very exciting to me. My mother has been doing it for years for me and my sister. To me she's a gypsy. She tells you things that you don't want to know. She doesn't try to sugarcoat anything. My mother tells it like she sees it. The things that she tells me make me feel upset, but in the end she is never wrong.

When she tells the fortune of other people she acts the same. She doesn't hide anything. Sometimes they just hang up the phone on her. She always says, "They wanted the truth, I gave them the truth, but really they didn't want the truth. They wanted me to tell a lie to them and tell them everything was great."

I Had My Fortune Told

Janice English
March 14, 2001

I have been studying astrology since 1967, and when you study astrology, just by association you usually read about other metaphysical subjects like tarot cards and numerology, among other things.

I met this woman in 1977, whose name was Sherry, who talked a lot about tarot cards. I had read a lot about tarot cards but had never had a reading. She talked about these cards, and I was fascinated by them.

One day a year later, the opportunity came for me to have a reading. The woman that I went to had a store on Lexington Avenue. As I walked up the stairs I wondered what I was getting into. The woman led me into a room and showed me the tarot cards. She proceeded to tell me I had a lot of problems in my life. She said I had the spirit of a German woman in my stomach, and that is the reason I was having these problems. She also said I would have a lot of female problems because of the spirit of the German woman in my stomach.

I thought the woman wasn't telling me the truth, but I didn't say anything. She told me if I came back with a tomato and a white handkerchief and more money she could remove the spirit from my stomach. Well, I paid the woman her fee and left, never to return. I left her store and went to a place called Weiser's Bookstore, where I bought my own deck of tarot cards and a book about them.

I now have been reading Tarot cards for the last twenty-three years. I read them professionally and personally. There is something about the cards that is honest and truthful. They give you clarity and they connect you to yourself in ways that most people are unaware of. They also keep you connected to a higher source, which some people call God. If not for that lady giving me such an awful reading, I might not be on the spiritual journey that I am now.

Define Divine

Muhammad Siagha
March 17, 2004

If I had to choose a number to define divine
I would choose the number one
If I had to choose a word to define divine
I would choose the word Me
If I had to choose a letter of the
Alphabet to define divine
I would choose the letter U

Peace thru Poetry
From Me to U
Muhammad Mosque #7
Harlem New York

Super Powers

Walter L. Schubert
May 1, 2003

In so many ways, to ask what I would want in the way of super powers is a waste of time, like asking oneself how one would live if one could live life all over again. But it is fun to wonder.

I was asked that question by a dating service. I answered that "I wished I could swing the hammer that would strike the blow that would clear up the mist of missed understandings." I was trying to impress my would-be dates.

I was also trying to tell my would-be dates that I was a writer, with some charisma, I hoped. So maybe, what I should have given as my wish to have super powers was simply to be a good writer—or to be a good date for the girl I was trying to impress.

I have since learned more about women who are impressed by such dramatic statements. When I have finished my masterpiece I find—too often—that what was intended as a message for the heart was received merely as an entertainment. So I was revealed to myself as an impostor, one at odds with himself, or—even worse—as a clown.

With one step backward I see now what I really want: I would like to be myself, to accept myself, and to feel accepted. This is as natural as looking through one's eyes and yet as impossible as seeing the back of one's head. It is the gift of grace that is rarer than radium, yet commoner than water. To be natural is to be blessed with a superior nature, to be at one with oneself. The most supernatural power of all is the power to do what comes naturally.

Part 3:

The Worst of Times

The Worst Night

Janice English
April 2, 2002

I'm sure most of us have had many worst nights of our lives, and I'm no different, but one of the worst nights of my life was when I had my daughter, Tia.

It was December 8, 1976. I was six months pregnant and under a lot of stress because I already had a child who was sick. I was living in my mother's apartment, and she was a bitch. I was having problems with Tia's father, who I realized would never amount to anything. I also wasn't taking care of myself properly. By that I mean, at that time in my life, I didn't understand about how diet and nutrition played a big part in the health of a baby.

I went to bed about eleven that night. I woke up about three in the morning with a pain. I turned on the light and thick clots of blood were between my legs. I was terrified. I had never seen such blood before. I called for my mother; she came and woke my sister Tina, and she helped me get dressed. Tina called a cab, and we sped off to the hospital. I thought I was going to die, because there was just too much blood.

I don't remember a lot, but I do remember people taking off my clothes and people running around. I remember being on the hospital table, and they were asking me questions. I also remember someone who I thought was a nurse holding my hand tightly. I looked up and all I could see were her eyes. She had on hospital scrubs, green with a green cap covering her head, just like you see on TV.

The next thing I knew I was above myself, looking down at myself and the doctors and nurses. I saw all of them. The doctor told me to wiggle my toes; he was screaming at me. I heard someone say, "We're losing her." I saw them stick something in my throat and I saw that someone still holding my hand.

Then I remember I was in the recovery room. My throat was hurting like hell. Someone I don't remember told me I had a daughter. She weighed two pounds and two ounces, and she was alive.

So, you see, the worst night of my life lasted three months while she was in the hospital fighting for her life. There are a lot of answers that I probably will never know. Like, who was that masked lady who held my hand? Was she an angel? Did I really leave my body? The staff kept telling me that they almost lost me. I asked one of the doctors why my throat hurt so bad. He told me that they had to stick a tube down my throat, because I had stopped breathing.

Thankfully, those days are over now. Tia is twenty-five years old and has given me two beautiful grandchildren—boys. I haven't had a worst night of my life in a very long time.

The Worst Night

Pierce McLoughlin
April 3, 2002

In 1979, I left the seminary and was back in New York City looking
for a job. Close friends had warned me where my drinking would leave
me. I dismissed the criticism and went on with my life.

A good Irish Catholic like me could not possibly be an alcoholic.
What would the family say? What would the church say? Might as
well be a pedophile.

The worst night of my life began at my brother's condo on the
Upper East Side. I had a couple six-packs of beer and left the resi-
dence to pick up vodka. Two bottles. It was about eleven.

I walked down to the East River and slowly polished off the
vodka. No ice, no water. After brooding for a while, I got up, took off
my parka and shoes, and jumped into the icy water—off a pier.
Joggers saw me in the water and called the police. I was fished out and
taken to Metropolitan Hospital where I remained for ten weeks.

While at the hospital, I cleaned up and began to remember the
warnings I had been given about booze. I saw the Thorazine shuffle
and Haldol shuffle firsthand. Finally, it sinks in. "Keep it simple, stupid. Don't drink, and go to meetings." AA meetings.

I was released in 1980 and began to put my life together all over
again. I got an apartment in the Bronx and started working with a
security firm. From there I branched out into other jobs, always keeping the focus on sobriety. Today, I have over twenty years clean. *One
day at a time.*

There was also a price to pay for drinking over fifteen years. My
brother and his wife have not contacted me in twenty years. My only
family today is the twelve-step program started by Bill Wilson and Dr.
Robert Smith seventy years ago.

The doctors at Metropolitan Hospital said it was miraculous that I had survived the East River in 1979. Doctors don't usually deal in miracles. The Higher Power made my path in life clear.

Don't Drink and Go To Meetings.

The Worst Night

Carol West
May 27, 1998

There have been nights when I've been sick when I thought it was the worst time of my life. Not being able to get to a drugstore, because I didn't have enough money for medicine or because I was coughing my guts out. Also, nights when I had just enough money to get home from a bad date. There have been times when I've wished I'd been able to buy food to fill an empty stomach so I could sleep and not worry about the fears of a day of life that gather in the mind at bedtime.

What I was never aware of, nor heard, was that the worst thing is not having the humanness of a body next to you as you journey through the darkest time of the day. The feel of someone to hold on to, to feel a life that cares, to have a union, not always sex, and a moment of laughter and understanding. Someone to make a cup of coffee for in the morning.

The worst night of my life is now, when I sleep alone.

The Worst Night

Nelson Blackman
May 27, 1998

My worst night was one Christmas Eve when I was a child. My mother and I had gone to see my sister, who lived on the Upper West Side. When we came home to Harlem, there was a huge fire. Red firetrucks were lined up and down 128th Street. The fire was in the apartment next door. It belonged to Dorothy, this nice church-going lady, who had accidentally left her stove on. She survived, but her place was wrecked. All our neighbors who lived in the building were standing outside. Everyone had been evacuated. We didn't know where my father was, we were so worried. It turned out he was asleep in the back room of our apartment. When we finally got back in we found him. My mother screamed at him, "There was a fire! Don't you know what's going on?" He was intoxicated, too much beer, so he missed the fire, the evacuation, the noise. He'd slept through the whole thing.

The Worst Day

Tory Connolly Walker
March 17, 2004

I was recently hired for a part-time promoter job for a morning newspaper and it was a worst-day/best-day scenario. I felt good and lousy
at the same time. First the sorta good. At nine dollars to thirteen dollars an hour, three hours a day, you couldn't beat it for freeing up time.
Time I need to prepare for ministry (on cable TV), a program called
Quest to Victory. It's now been ten years that I've been preparing. This is
no overnight calling. First the Lord had to rid me of the voices in my
head that started twenty-five years before. Then I had to learn to listen to the insistent voice of God. After that I had to "try the spirits,"
as the Bible says, and make sure that the voice of the Holy Spirit
indeed was the Lord's, because the devil is very crafty. Finally I had to
obey the Lord's voice and ask Christ to lead me daily. Deliverance is
an inside job.

My outside job is for *AM New York*, a colorful paper with pithy
news stories and witty writing. It's a good quick morning read. I've
received compliments from folks who enjoy it. As a promoter, my job
is a euphemism for "hawker" or "barker." I like to call myself "promoter." My husband says woman-with-journalism-degree-who-
passes-out-papers. (He recently got laid off from his job, and now he
is a man-with-art-aspirations-who-passes-out-papers.) I don't
"hawk," which to me would amount to screeching "Extra! Extra!
Read all about it!" 1930's style. I don't bark, which would put off the
average would-be reader—even the transit cop's dog would be taken
aback by my barking. I say, "Good morning, *AM New York* news, free
paper, Wednesday edition. Is it love for Serena? Everyone wants to
know." "*AM New York*, well written and to the point, save money at
the newsstand. Thank you. Donald Trump is auditioning for the next

Apprentice. Read all about it." "Good morning, *AM New York.* Always free. Save time. Save money. Hi! Here you go, have a great day. Good morning."

Did I mention what was lousy? Sometimes a voice creeps back—the one that with a chorus of chaotic voices once drove me crazy (literally). This time I knew how to say, "Be gone in Jesus's name!" But it's a common voice. Most of us hear it through the day. Some call it "toxic self talk." I still call it Satan. This one day, the devil was on a roll. I heard over and over, "Look at you! Graduate of Ohio State University. Former news reporter and your illustrious journalism career has been reduced to passing out papers! Well, you did get back in journalism, ha-ha-ha-ha! Didn't you do something similar to this in grade school? Weren't you a papergirl at ten years old? Now you're in your forties, and you're back to being a paper girl." "Shut up!" I said, almost audibly. A woman who had her hand out to receive a paper recoiled and scurried by paper-free. The voice finally did stop when I heard the Lord say, "Why not use your job as research? Yes, study the symphony of New Yorkers who parade past you daily and use them to write an article about the readers and submit it to *AM New York.*" The devil was outdone by the Lord but not before erupting in garbled curses. Then it was gone. The voice banished. I could hear myself say, "Good Morning! *AM New York!*" I smiled and the man taking the paper smiled back. "Good read!" he said. "Thank you," I smiled, as the sun actually seemed to break through the ceiling of the subway.

Homeless

Ronnie Eisen
March 27, 2002

In 1977, I had entered the shelter system for approximately one month. Christmas was approaching, and I could not bear the idea that I must spend this day in the women's shelter. I was broke and completely miserable.

I went to the phone booth and dialed the toll-free number for battered women. They told me they had room for me at Mother Theresa's, and I could move in on Saturday afternoon. You can't imagine how happy I was to be going away from the shelter.

I carefully packed my few belongings, leaving a few things behind for my new friends, Crystal and Mickey. I never told my counselor where I was going. I left him a note, thanking him for all his help. Then I just left, pretending to be going to the laundry.

I rode the train to Harlem with great happiness. The convent was even better than I thought it would be. We had no Christmas tree yet, but Mother put one up and let us all decorate it. We helped cook all the meals and cleaned the place. For once, there was no smoking and no violence. I really enjoyed the peace and quiet.

But then, the annoying thing happened. It was Christmas Day, and Mother told us we had to leave at eight in the morning and not come back until four in the afternoon. I had gotten sick at the party the night before, and I felt awful. I had no money at all and nowhere to go. Having never been in Manhattan on Christmas Day before, I imagined nothing would be open, I would freeze and die.

Suddenly, I remembered a story in the newspaper about Holy Apostles Church. I got a copy of the *Tablet* and checked the address. A Nigerian woman told me they would be serving Christmas dinner there. She too had no place to go. We made our way down from

Harlem in the snow. We attended church at Holy Apostles, and then went to the meal.

Everyone was nice to us, and several men gave us referrals to other soup kitchens that I have been going to ever since. I thank God for all the nice people I have met, and all the help they have given me.

My friend was able to reunite with her sister and find work in America. I'm still homeless, but I do work now and go to Holy Apostles whenever I can.

Homelessness

Bill Acheson
April 4, 2001

Today as I was walking here, I was thinking about my situation. Good if I win a bed at the Rescue Mission lottery tonight, bad if I don't. I had a few good months at Greenpoint, Brooklyn, with my own private room and a set of keys; a shared apartment with aquarium, plants, dog, and back garden. But we had to leave the place.

I seem to be adjusting, enjoying this adventure in unstable housing. "Why is this?" I was wondering as I walked. Seems I feel connected—I like people most times. Homeless people are good people—we are people—we are very real, no phonies here. We are direct, almost a military bluntness, as I remember those days. Just mind my own business and don't push into one another's private space—just some respect, please.

In addition to feeling connected (not alone, isolated, a victim of society and my own life), I see some hope in my present situation. It is not forever, my basic needs are taken care of. I have learned to survive on little, on the basics. Can I survive today only spending twenty-five cents for a banana and forty-two cents for a McDonald's senior coffee? Probably.

Saw my cardiologist yesterday. Things seem to be in control. Yes, there is hope. Even if things turn bleak, I rely on God for eternal hope. The apostle Paul states, and I believe, "All things work for the good, for those who believe." Paul's suffering, and Christ's, was definitely worse than my own discomforts.

Homelessness

Thyatira English
April 2, 2002

December 21, 2000, was the night my mother, sister, nephews, and I entered the shelter system. We had to go to this place called EAU,* altogether as one family, but when we got there they split us up. My sister and nephews went together, and they tried to send my mother and me to a women's shelter because they felt that I wasn't a child. After the lady spoke to someone else, they didn't split my mother and me up. But we were still to be split from my sister and nephews.

We had to wait and be called for an "overnight." My mother and I got called, but my sister didn't. So she was upset. When we left for the overnight, we were scared and didn't know what to expect. We went to this place called Powers, which was very cold. I think we got there at 4 a.m. They woke us up at 8 a.m. to get ready to go back to the EAU. They have these buses to come and get you from Powers to go to EAU. When you get to EAU you give them your papers so they know that you're in, and you wait for them to call you. This could be an all-day process.

You wait for them to call you. They serve this horrible food that didn't sit too well in my stomach. After you talk to them, you wait for a placement. If they don't find you a placement, you go to another overnight, which we did.

In the morning, we missed the bus that could take us back to EAU, so we had to take a cab. We got there, and I saw my sister and nephews. They had gotten a place all the way in Queens. We got placed in Manhattan, which separated us from each other. My sister never had to move back in—she was in Queens; that was it. For us, it wasn't the same. We were found ineligible—we still had to move every twenty-eight days, because we were adults. It was like that for us until

April 2001, when we moved to this place called Auburn. When we were in EAU, we heard so many bad things about Auburn that we didn't want to go, but we had no choice.

My worst night lasted for fourteen months.

*Emergency Assistance Unit

Song of Homeless Writers

Walter L. Schubert
May 7, 2003

Out of the long winter's night
We have assembled to write,
So that the world might know
To home we must go.

So exchange, for a change,
Your money for a chance
To send us on our way in a verbal dance
To home we must go.

Always on the run,
Hallelujah, I'm a bum!
Got plenty of nothing but God's only Son
To home we must go.

Everyone has a story to tell,
I think that we each tell it well.
Now, here is one you don't already know:
To home we must go.

We, having no money,
Exchange stories that are funny.
But others are bad and will send you home mad.
To home we must go.

Pillars of the community have a tired old song:
"You must have done something wrong."
But sell out that high, so our low you may buy:
To home we must go.

Final Eviction

George Glass
March 24, 2004

The deliciousness of autumn still permeated the lawns of ancient Greenwich Village. Samantha, the superintendent of an aging building on Perry Street, had two days left before her final eviction from the premises. Not a soul telephoned her, none of her friends or colleagues returned her dignified appeals for help vis-à-vis emails she had sent.

Her cuticles were a concern to her because she had conditioned her body into expecting monthly manicures. Now there was no money for manicures. It would be frivolous to explain this to anyone, she understood. However, as the skin grew unkempt over the base of her fingernails, it did so in a fashion that made it grotesquely impossible to successfully wear nail polish.

Without nail polish, she felt she had no appeal. The nail polish she wore like a foundation enabled her color-blind eyesight to mix and match different pieces of clothing she possessed as a former burlesque dancer. Now everything was out of whack. It was as if she were "disconnected from her life."

She had been presented with few choices in the forty-eight hours before she was to become a homeless person. She bought a Buick Celebrity a fortnight before with the six hundred dollars she received, in twenty-dollar bills, from the remaining jewelry she had kept from her husband. It would be difficult to consolidate all of her children's toys, her parents' wedding gifts, and all the souvenirs of her loved ones and the many periods of her life.

Uncannily, she stepped on a flyer while crossing Gansevoort Street. It asked for help in locating one of the missing members of the Imperial Court of New York City. It made her remember, through the conduction of her thought patterns, that she could always have a meal at the church up on Ninth Avenue, Holy Apostles.

Employed but Homeless

Donald Mackey
February 1, 1995

After working several months, I moved to an efficiency apartment in the Bronx and I bought a new wardrobe. It had not taken me long to readjust to the world of work. One day, as I stood at my office window and watched the busy Park Avenue traffic of employed people going to and fro, I thought, "Wow, I actually moved from park bench to Park Avenue." I felt secure. I was employed by a company that had been in business since 1906.

By the end of the year, I had high expectations for continued success. There was a lavish New Year's party at the office. The boss gave each employee Chandon Imperial Champagne. The bottle was covered with a red carnation stuck on at the neck of the bottle. After the office party I went to visit my mother in New Jersey. I gave her my bottle of champagne and returned to New York. The office was closed for the holidays until January 4, which was payday. Savoring my first paycheck in the New Year, I opened the envelope, removed the check, and read the letter that was attached.

It was a pink slip regretfully informing me that the following week would be my last week of employment. The letter complimented my outstanding service to the company and noted that due to circumstances beyond its control, the doors would have to close.

Cleaning out my desk was one of the hardest things that I ever had to do. Two weeks after I had left the company, I was asked if I wanted to return to work with a skeleton crew on a part-time basis until the company closed. I accepted, because I had not yet found another job. Now that I was receiving only part-time wages, I was falling behind with my rent. The landlord was not interested in cooperating with me. He was leaving me messages under my door, but he never returned my calls. The opportunity to work part-time at the office helped to ease my transition back to being unemployed again. After working until 9 p.m. through an exhausting day of handling dusty portable files, I returned to my apartment in the Bronx. I found that the landlord had changed the lock on my door. I went to the building superintendent who allowed me to go into the apartment to get some of my things. I packed all that I could carry into a large suitcase and left. Refusing to return to a homeless men's shelter, I sat on a park bench all night. Agonized, I sat alone in silence. I dared not wonder how much worse things could be.

I paced back and forth in front of the park bench, staring at my suitcase and thinking about the things that I had left back at my apartment. I knew, as day was breaking, that I would not want to spend another night outdoors if I could help it. I could not live with my mother, because the senior citizens building where she lived would not allow it. Besides, I felt that I wanted to be alone in my misery. Later that evening, I returned to the East River Men's Shelter. I was fortunate enough to be assigned a bed. The shelter employees who were working in the intake office knew me from before. For them it was routine; they expect the men who live there to return sooner or later.

This time the elevator was working. I took it to the fifth floor and stopped to use the restroom on the way to my bed. A security guard stopped me. She told me that I could not go into the restroom just then, but I could go to another floor or come back in twenty minutes. I later learned that a young man had been found dead, lying on the shower room floor. He had a heart attack while smoking crack cocaine. Exhausted, I entered my room and immediately began placing my possessions into the footlocker at the foot of my bed. Just as I finished and sat on my bed with my back to the wall to think, one of the shelter residents opened a fire exit door that was directly across from my room. I watched from my opened door as he was sneaking a friend of his into the building. When he opened the fire exit door, he set off the burglar alarm. The alarm sounded for at least an hour before being shut off. The restroom was now reopened for use; I had watched as EMS carried the body bag past the door of my room. I went to the restroom to stuff some dampened toilet tissue into my ears, to help muffle the piercing sound of the burglar alarm. As I stood looking into the mirror at the sink, I could see the chalk outline where the body had lain on the shower room floor. Near the outline of his hand and arm was a book of matches, a pencil, several pennies, and sticks of chewing gum.

I returned to my room and closed the door behind me. The burglar alarm was suddenly turned off. There was silence. Just as I was beginning to appreciate the quiet, the usual shelter noises began creeping back. The population of the shelter was eight hundred men. At any given time the sounds that were prevalent were the rattling sound of metal garbage can lids; loud banging on room doors; echoing shouts up and down the hallways; and the sounds of gagging, vomiting, spitting, nose blowing, and fighting.

I wished that I still had a room with a view of the East River. Instead I was now looking from a window on the west side of the building, three floors lower. It faced a courtyard area, which contained a two-story building complex extending from the main building to the center of the courtyard. My window was two floors above the roof of this complex. As I stooped and looked out the window, I saw the occasional flurry of used toilet paper, food, and gum wrappers tossed from windows above. Now and then an unwanted article of too-dirty clothing would come floating by the window, which had the appearance of a body falling. Except for the occasional splash of urine rain thrown down from a bottle by someone who did not want to use the bathroom, it would sometimes almost look like the cascade of a ticker-tape parade. I watched a prophylactic land on my windowsill. It slithered off the edge of the windowsill and fell to the roof below. I turned from the window. I would rather look at the blank walls, the ceiling, and the floor.

After a while, the man who slept in the bed across from me came into the room. He picked up a newspaper from the floor beside his bed, sat down, and placed the paper in his lap. I spoke to him. I told him that a mouse had been crawling around inside the palm of his upturned glove that lay on the floor. I told him that the mouse had also crawled on his scarf of folded toilet paper, which was also on the floor. I told him that the mouse had crawled all over his eyeglasses as the mouse nibbled on his cookies. As the man put on his eyeglasses, he answered, "Yeah, I know, mice around here do things like that."

I thought that I had seen my last mouse story my first time around the shelter, when the man across from me had caught two mice on a sticky trap under his bed. It was two in the morning, when I and two other men asked him to get rid of the mice. He said he was not yet ready to get out of bed. He would not allow anyone else to reach under his bed in order to dispose of the mice. We had to spend the rest of the night listening to the sounds of their squeaking.

I watched my roommate remove a cookie from the pack that the mouse had eaten from. Bewildered, I went to bed and turned my back to him. I looked out of the window and noticed that the sky was clear. The moon was full and bright. I decided to study the view of the moon until I fell asleep. I would look at the moon with one eye open and the other eye closed. Then I would switch sides. It seemed that one eye was telescopic and the other was microscopic. But that also seemed to alternate. In all the years past, I had never looked at the moon for more than a glimpse.

The next morning I walked to the east side of the building and watched the sunrise. During breakfast in the mess hall, I put the frozen cup of juice I had been given into my cup of coffee to thaw out. I accidentally dropped my roll on the table. I would not eat it, because I remembered having seen a cafeteria worker sweep off a tabletop with the push broom that he had used to sweep the floor. After breakfast, everyone had to line up to take a picture for security

ID. This decision was made because of the young man who was found dead the day before. He had sneaked into the building illegally.

Later, as I was taking a shower, I noticed that the debris I had seen around the chalk outline of the body was still there. By this time, a pool of water had collected on the floor. There were no curtains. One of the community service workers came into the shower room to mop. But he changed his mind. Instead he came back with a push broom. He pushed all the water out of the shower room, spreading it up and down the hallways to give the impression that he had mopped. He pushed the debris that the dead man had left up and down the hallways; it seemed as if he was sweeping death all over the building. When I was preparing to leave the shower room, I asked the man who was taking a shower if he wanted me to close the door to the room, which the service worker had left propped open with a garbage can. He answered yes. I turned back and pushed the can with my foot. The bottom of the can caught on one of the loose tiles and tumbled over to the floor, spilling much of the garbage inside. I was not the only one who used my feet to touch things in the shelter. Many men were in the habit of even using their feet to flush the toilet; it was often too filthy to touch.

This time around at the shelter I'm going back to the drawing board, to where the employment notices are posted. I know that there is another job out there for me. I know that I will never find it by just standing and looking out my shelter window.

So I Lied

Joe Negrelli
March 17, 2004

Shortly after I had my bypass operation I was given extreme kindness by some do-gooder who took pity on a very frail old man. I was given American Ballet Theater tickets, first mezzanine, first row.

After watching a good performance of *Swan Lake* (not the best I'd ever seen) I engaged in banter during the intermission regarding the performance. I was asked about my ballet knowledge and cultural references.

I cheerfully told the small group of about ten people that I had indeed seen the great Margot Fonteyn and the semi-great Rudolf Nureyev dance this same ballet, and although good, nothing this evening compared to that performance forty years before.

There were literally hundreds of questions regarding both performances and performers, my ideas and/or observations. Then came personal questions regarding my social background. Where and with which family I was brought up. Where I was raised. Till finally, we got to education and I am not sure why (yes I really am) I decided to lie.

I told them I had private tutors until high school and then on to college. It's true my college has got a very good academic reputation, but I again stretched the truth more than a little. My saving grace was intermission was over. Saved by the dimming and raising lights of the attractive chandeliers at the Met. My next saving grace was I had to run after the performance to catch a bus to go home.

Yes, so I lied; I know it's not my first, but I do pray that I can learn to live without embellishing the truth so blatantly.

So I Lied

Carol West
March 17, 2004

My first lessons were the Ten Commandments, especially "Thou shalt not lie," number eight on the list. If my grandmother caught anyone in a lie, she would say, "Liar, liar, pants on fire." My mother would advise, "You shouldn't tell untruths." Father B said, "God always knows when you lie." A friar preached, "Why is a 'little lie' always white?"

The nuns at school would make me write a minimum of one hundred times, "I will not lie," or, if the fib warranted, the offender was whacked with a two-foot wooden pointer that Sister always waved indiscriminately at the class.

I learned not so much to lie, but with flowery speech weave around the topic, gloss over the subject, or be kind. To friends with fashion disasters, I say, "Isn't that sweet." To hair mistakes, I've learned to keep silent. If covering up an untruth, I embroider my words to a new topic. On government forms if you make a mistake or can't remember, is it a lie?

The worst thing I could say or think about me is "so I lied."

So I Lied

Norman Clayton
April 19, 2004

The marriage of
The farmer in the dell
To Goldilocks is my
Own invention

It could be worse
I could have her marry
Count Dracula but I won't
I'm a realist ideally

As a farmer's wife Goldilocks
Could learn how to milk cows
And collect eggs. She would lose
Some of her pickiness

Does Cinderella really need
A prince? He could turn out
To be Dracula but
That's another story

Me and My Big Mouth

Bill Acheson
April 11, 2001

Germs, germs, germs. All over New York City. That's what me and my big mouth are into these days.

Last week I had this little tickle in my throat that turned into a drippy, messy nose. The last two days, this cold has developed into a strong, loud cough. An inconvenience to me as I lose sleep, an inconvenience to other people as they feel threatened by my germs.

Comments from the cold front:

"Cover your mouth." (But my mouth is covered, I thought.)

"Sorry," I said.

"Cover your mouth." (But my nose is also gushing and messy, and I am trying to find a tissue.)

"Sorry," I said.

"Cover your mouth, bullet-nose!" (Time for me to move away fast.)

Others say nothing and uncomfortably shift away. Still others have a bored, stoic response, as if this is normal in New York City— probably my response in their situation.

Soon this cold will disappear. I will have other opportunities to exert my right to be a minor pest to others as they return, in kind, their irritating behavior to me, in this hotbed of overpopulation.

Me and My Big Mouth

Pierce McLoughlin
April 11, 2001

I thought I'd write on this, since I do not really have a big mouth.

In the 1950s, as a kid in grade school I was very much a wall-flower. Tragically, my dad did little to help. He had his own problems as a functioning alcoholic. My home life was fairly stable because of my mother. She was a college graduate and an assistant editor with *America* magazine, published by Jesuits.

The only time I may have been perceived as a big mouth was when I was drinking. Sometimes, I might say something stupid to a girl or person in a bar (enter the demon—alcohol) and ruin my chances for a date or relationship.

I would shrug it off in my alcoholic persona (arrogance), believing I had a lifetime to meet the right girl (more alcoholic idiocy). I'm sure people around me wanted to help, but I never gave them an opening to try and reach me.

When I was labeled an ignorant Irish drunk and expelled from the seminary in 1979, I knew my big mouth was involved. Enter true humility (a desire to do God's will). After twenty years as a "recovering drunk," I am now living a beautiful life. Minus a big mouth.

My Most Humiliating Moment

Nelson Blackman
March 8, 2000

It happened around three years ago when I was on my way downtown and couldn't pay my fare. I didn't have enough money for both lunch and transportation from 125th Street to Chambers Street, but I had to get to work. I was a janitor at the Family Courthouse. I went down the stairs, and the A train was in the station. I jumped the turnstile and got on the train. The doors closed. Then a police officer halted the train. "You with the purple Lakers jacket," he said, pointing to me. He told me to get off the train. It was rush hour, so the train was packed. Everyone was staring at me. I felt like sinking into the ground. He gave me a ticket for a fifty-dollar fine, then he let me back on the train. I paid the fare and made it to work by nine. I jumped the turnstiles a few times after that. What can I say? I'm rebellious.

The Most Humiliating Thing

John Cabello
April 14, 2004

My son starting grammar school, once
In a misunderstanding, looked at me from top
To feet exclaiming "Aaah, people of different
Cultures!" and turned his back on me, leaving
Me alone in his room, petrified. Before I could
Run to hug him, cover him with kisses, fill him
With daddy's love, he ran inside the room again.
Jumping to my breast, he wet my face with his
Hot tears flooding. He yelled at me, repentant.
"Sorry, Dad. I didn't mean it." Both him and me
Were reawakened to a better stage of our shared
Life, each of us the other's most humiliating thing,
Alive in our minds, just two real men on earth.

My Most Humiliating Moment

Tory Connolly Walker
April 14, 2004

I have a top-ten list of most humiliating moments. Sort of like David Letterman's countdown to shame. The moment that comes immediately to mind was during my senior year at Ohio State University. There I was all set to graduate, but not before causing my father (who was footing most of my college expenses) some angst and my mother a mixture of I'm-not-sure-what since she always seemed more like an older sister.

At the time I was submitting stories to the college paper, *The Lantern*, and getting published there and on a student "fringe" paper, *Our Choking Times*. I wrote from the soul, all in preparation for my coming career in journalism before I got sidetracked, at least for the summer of '77. A friend of a friend, a concert promoter, borderline dirty old man (he was late forties, which at twenty-one seemed pretty ancient, but now that I am late forties seems positively in the prime of life). This guy submitted my name to a contest, then told my friend that I'd be perfect and with some coaching could probably win.

It was a beauty contest but sort of an invented one for publicity to launch the concert and promote the hit record *du jour*. The hit song was "Brick House" by the Commodores, one of Motown's hottest groups, and the contest was for Miss Columbus (Ohio) Brick House (they were supposed to have them in every city). The winner at the national level would also win a movie role with Billy Dee Williams in his next film. I was jazzed. Fifteen girls competed at a popular dance club, sort of Miss America–style in swimsuits and heels and then revealing their "intellect" or "wit" when asked a serious question. To be honest, there was a girl who was a brick-house bombshell with an eye-popping figure (judging by the collective stares of the gentlemen in the audience), but the dear bombshell was dumb as a bag of hammers! I was pretty adept at stringing a sentence together, and she fumbled through her name. Since they wanted a kind of spokesmodel winner, I won. Sharon (the bombshell) became the runner-up and we became fast friends, since the Commodores' management closed down the contest at that point and picked the two of us to go on tour together.

We won gift certificates and free travel, limo rides, meals, money for clothes. We stood behind barricades in record stores in swimsuits, high heels, and fake furs and signed autographs along with the Commodores. I always wore a pair of slacks over my swimsuit in public because I didn't want to look slutty—and yes, I was against nudity. Sharon and I roomed together, giggled, gossiped, and drank champagne while we traveled to Hartford, Connecticut; Philadelphia; Boston; and made a pit stop in Dayton before the tour was to have a huge concert at Madison Square Garden.

It was at a packed arena in Dayton, Ohio. Sharon and I were "anointed" stage dancers on the tour, and we were ecstatic to be onstage with Lionel Richie and the Commodores. We strutted out from opposite ends of the stage to the Commodores' "She's a Brick House—she's a mighty mighty . . ." Sharon danced solo, then I danced solo. Suddenly a "boo" erupted from the back while the spotlight was on me. Half of the ten thousand people packed in the arena began booing in a huge roar for a full five minutes. I was mortified and finally stumbled offstage when the song was over, almost tripping over my too-high heels. I ran into the photographer who was stage side, who would become one of my best friends over the years.

"Why did they boo?" I broke out in sobs. I was thinking I did my best Chaka Khan dance moves. Chuckie laughed.

"I was in the back of the arena earlier," he said, "and I heard loud protests, people complaining Miss Brick House is white! Then everyone started booing, not even knowing why they were booing," said Chuckie. "Just really stupid."

"But I'm not white! I'm a Black woman, a light-skinned Black woman." (African-American was not yet in vogue.)

"Oh, of course I can see that," said Chuckie, "but way in the back with bright lights washing out your skin tone and the fact that you wear that straightened Farrah Fawcett–looking hairdo—well, I guess they just couldn't tell."

Today, of course, things like this don't matter. Eminem is one of the biggest rap stars, and Halle Berry has crossed the color line for actresses playing parts that are not race specific. But to be booed by ten thousand people in a roar of disapproval made me wish the earth would open up and swallow me whole, no matter what the reason.

I went on to work at Motown in Los Angeles, and Lionel Richie would come through and "razz me" to my ongoing mortification. "Be nice to her. That's Miss Columbus Brick House!" he teased to the staff. While I was there, Teena Marie, a Caucasian singer, became an R&B queen, and I bought all her albums, shaking my head sometimes thinking how crazy show business can be and how fickle the fans. I'm no longer in show business and that's one reason why, but I still have fond memories. I last found my Miss Brick House trophy in my mother's basement, not black or white but faded gold.

The Most Humiliating Thing That Ever Happened to Me

Norman Clayton
April 14, 2004

The most humiliating thing that ever happened to me was being born. I did not ask for it. I was safe, secure, and sound where I was. I thought I was home. It felt like home. I had lived there for nine full months. I was happy. I got everything I thought I needed. So what's with the eviction? And they were rough about it. When I finally left, under protest, they spanked the bee-Jesus out of me. Then I got to eat and things were better but not right. They wrapped me up. In protest, I peed. That will show them! And the outside was light and it held big grown-up faces. They all had grins, shitty grins, so I shit on them. But they didn't mind—which was the most asinine thing that happened.

I thought, "Fuck them if they can't take a joke." And Mother smiled as if agreeing. I hope she can take a joke. I hope she can't take a joke. It's humiliating either way. Too bright, too cold, too warm. Anyway, I'm here and I still don't like it one bit. I just wanna go home.

My Most Humiliating Moment

Leucio Parella
April 14, 2004

I have something to tell you. What I am about to tell you was so devastating to me that it took a long time to share it with you. I was not only affected emotionally, but it has stressed me and affected me physically.

I am not here to put the blame on anyone. What happened already happened. Now here goes. When I was seven I was raped, and when I was nine I was almost kidnapped. These two incidents took place at the Callahan-Kelly Playground.

The rape took place at the back of the handball court. I was in the park playing. Then Angelo told me to do what he asked me to do. I replied with this answer, "NO. I am not doing that." He responds with if I don't do what he asked me to do he'd hurt me. That moment I still replied, "NO." Then he told me that he would punch me. That moment I lost control of myself with who I am. I was threatened. Soon after the act, I went home. I felt humiliated and hurt. When I was a teenager, I knew what was the meaning of rape. In my mature years, I learned about past issues with sexual abuse.

The kidnapping took place at the front of the park by the flagpole. On the way to our parents' home, I was on the sidewalk at Eastern Parkway between Fulton Street and Truxton Street. I had a white short-sleeve shirt with navy pants. A man approached me and asked me where the direction of this place was. The man was about thirty years old. He had with him a notepad, papers, and pencil. I told him, "Sorry, I don't know where it is." Then he showed me his vehicle and he said, "Come on, I'll show you the way."

His car was parked across the street from the address of a girl that I knew. Her name was Helen. She was the one who I give jewelry to.

We went in the car. Soon after, he started to use bad language. I told him to drop me off. The car took off. Shortly he told me very abruptly that he would give me a quarter if I would tell him how big my penis was in bad language. I was persistent in telling him I want to get out of the car. However, he drove around the park, and then he stopped on the side of the park on Fulton Street. He chose this area of the street for the same reason. He did not want people to know what he was up to. Before I got out of the car he asked the same question. For some reason I was calm about it. As a result I got out of the car, upset and outraged.

I went home traumatized. If I would tell this drama to our parents it would be devastating to Mom. If our father found out, he would have been angry with me. He had a short fuse. Besides, how could I say something like this to our parents, someone who has a disability like me? Keep in mind it always stays with me forever.

The Worst Advice I Ever Got

Peter Nkruma
April 30, 1999

The worst advice I ever got was "to thine own self be true." That advice came from William Shakespeare, through the voice of Hamlet. Shakespeare was playing fast and loose with the truth. What possible benefits are there to being true to thyself?

How many presidents achieved the presidency by being true to themselves? Candidates lie with a sly wink and a firm handshake. The candidate who manufactures the slickest image, and lies to the largest number of people best, wins.

Hamlet would not have stood a chance running for dogcatcher, much less president. But, of course, this advice was not meant to be taken as a road map for financial or political gain. To do that, one must summon up all the virtues of the underworld.

To treat every person one comes across as one treats oneself seems the key to emotional happiness. "To thine own self be true," is the worst advice I ever got for living, but maybe the best advice for drama. If I am true to myself, there exists no tension: I am me.

Worst Advice I Ever Got

Norman Clayton
May 9, 2004

The worst advice I ever got was from my father, who told me "Stay single." Until recently I was in my own ego-cocoon. I was in "I," as in the phrase "I want." But this prevented me from realizing I was selfish and lonely. It told me I was warm, loving, and giving, when I was not. It took a twelve-step program to teach me about sharing. I have no girlfriend now, but I am shopping. For once I won't be superficial in my declarations of love. It is time to grow up. My father died twenty years ago. I wrote him a letter once, accusing him of not loving any of his kids. He wrote back and said that he did love us. I felt elated. Then I told him I loved him and didn't love him at the same time. Like him, I was ambivalent.

A Job I'm Glad I Lost

Thyatira English
March 28, 2001

A job I'm glad I lost was a UPS job. I hated working there so much. When I first started I thought it would be all right. UPS gives all these benefits, you know, so I really wanted to work there. They said it was seasonal work, but if I did a good job it could be permanent.

I came in on time like I was supposed to. They worked me very hard. At UPS they have next-day delivery so around 9 p.m. they make you go faster. Basically, they treat you like you're a machine. See, I hadn't had many jobs before, so I wasn't used to the way people treat you when you work for them. At UPS if you hurt yourself, they asked you if you could still work. They didn't care about your health.

After I saw how they treated you, I didn't want to be permanent anymore. People think that UPS pays all this money, but they don't. If you're not a driver, you aren't making a lot of money. I was a loader/unloader. I worked only three, maybe four hours and was making $8.50 an hour, and it wasn't enough for me.

I was unhappy working there and couldn't wait until it was over. People tell me you're always going to get a job where people don't care about you. I refuse to believe people don't care about each other in a job, because I know there are some who do.

The Worst Job I Ever Had

Peter Nkruma
April 16, 2003

The worst job I ever had was doing data entry for the Department of Transportation. I had just turned eighteen, and was at the beginning of my life as an adult. My job was to enter into the DOT computers the auto-related deaths for the year 1987.

It is remarkable how many people die in auto-related deaths in New York. What is even more remarkable is the way in which officers describe the accidents in their police reports. The language is bureaucratic: "Victim crossed the intersection on a red light. Hit by minivan. Pronounced dead at 10:08." That sort of thing.

In the police reports there is an invariable Polaroid of the scene. Broken glass. Uprooted stop signs. Police tape. All of the accidents that I entered into the DOT computers involved no charges being pressed. I always wondered how a person could go on and resume his or her life after killing somebody—even if it was an accident. In 1987 there were many such people.

Back then, the DOT was just beginning to enter the digital age. The computers were ancient by today's standards. My space was in the corner of the eighth floor of a nondescript building next to City Hall. The walls were heavy, like a castle, and there were only a couple of windows. The atmosphere was like a Kafka novel. I quit two months later. I wonder who is doing that job now?

Band of Brothers

Pierce McLoughlin
May 8, 2002

One thing I learned very fast when I became a veteran was that you can't explain to civilians what it's like, if you were never in a uniform yourself. I was in the navy from 1968 to 1972.

It is a little like being in the Mob. Only this mob tries to do good in America. Of course, there are the usual flubs and screw-ups, but overall, the job gets done, no matter how dirty. No matter the loss of personnel.

I feel we can be grateful that we held together as a nation for two hundred years. You can see this during the Civil War. The government's primary purpose during the war was the preservation of the Union. During the conflict, we lost nearly 40 percent of the male population, both North and South.

I believe that Admiral Yamamoto described us as a "sleeping giant." He knew what we could achieve when Japanese military people thought us lazy and arrogant in 1941. Enter, also, bin Laden on 9/11.

Today, I think we are struggling against an enemy closer to home—poverty. My own feeling is that the American dollar is not worth the paper it is printed on. Corporate America is pushing the envelope and something is going to burst.

We will eventually come to terms with a more sane economy, but it will take three to five years before some leader will even out the capitalist playing field. The alternative is possibly another Hitler in America.

Hopefully, God will put together another "band of brothers" to stave off anarchy, death, or the dissolution of our nation.

Working for My Welfare

Donald Mackey

I am a participant in New York City's Work Experience Program, which requires welfare recipients to work for their monthly checks and food stamps. I am a fifty-year-old divorced man with five dependent children I want to support. I am ready and willing to work. I think the city's program is basically fair, though it has some problems that need to be ironed out.

I have had full-time jobs for more than thirty-five years, earning as much as forty-seven thousand dollars a year. I have been an employment interviewer for the New Jersey Department of Labor, a control-room operator for the Passaic Valley Sewage Commission, and an employment counselor at a private school in Manhattan.

But my life took an unfortunate turn after a serious back injury. I lost a job I loved—the one with the New Jersey labor department. I ended up on drugs and in a homeless shelter. I regret that chain of events, but with the help of my church, counseling, and a writing workshop, I quit cold turkey and have been clean for three years. I rent a room in a brownstone in Brooklyn and receive $256 a month in welfare and food stamps.

I do not want to be an anonymous welfare statistic. I want more than anything to earn an honest living again, perhaps as a coordinator of church-related community programs. I have a lot to offer.

Looking for a decent job, I sent out many resumes, but got no response. In February, the Work Experience Program assigned me and about thirty other welfare recipients between the ages of twenty and sixty to a sanitation garage in Brooklyn.

The first day, I was given a broom and a dustpan and told I would be putting in sixteen hours a week cleaning the garage. I couldn't hang up my coat because I shared a locker with nine other crewmembers, and it was already jammed with bottles of cleaning solution, toilet brushes, and a plunger. The lock was broken. I couldn't put my bag lunch in the refrigerator because the full-time garbage men had padlocked it.

The next day I asked for a pair of gloves, but they didn't have any. When I said it was important because I had injured my hand at home, I was given a dirty, used pair. I was afraid my hand would get infected.

After a month, I was told that I would be working sixteen hours a week outside, sweeping the streets. When I asked for a dust mask, I was told they were on order. I was issued an army jacket, a knit cap, and a new pair of gloves but wore my own sneakers because they were out of boots. Each morning we walked with our equipment to a cleaning area more than a mile away.

The program is intended to help thirty thousand inexperienced workers enter the job force. The goal for 1999 is one hundred thousand. It's a great idea that I hope will get and keep many New Yorkers off welfare. Yet in the rush to put people to work, confusion has ensued. The workfare program doesn't consider experience or education. I wish it provided for age and skill. And I wish the hours were more consistent. Now, for example, I am working twenty-four hours a week.

A woman I know had to stop going to college classes in order to get to her work assignment. A homeless man didn't come back to the garage because there was no place for him to shower. Full-time sanitation workers fear and resent us, because they are afraid we'll steal their jobs.

The Work Experience Program has gotten some things right. We can take a day off to interview for jobs, as long as we present written verification, and some supervisors seem to be sincerely trying to help. I just hope the program will turn out to be a concerted effort to aid those who want to work, not just a political Band-Aid.

Published in *The New York Times*, April 24, 1997

Good Cop, Bad Cop

Nelson Blackman
April 4, 2001

Bad cop: When I was homeless, five years ago, I had nowhere to go but the subway. I could only sleep for twenty minutes at a time. Cops harassed people sleeping on the train. I remember one cop who banged his nightstick against the seat and said, "Come on, let's go buddy."

Good cop: As a freelance photographer I recently took pictures of Isaac Hayes, the bald-headed *Shaft* star, for *The Bronx Times*. Hayes was at the Barnes & Noble in Baychester Avenue in Co-op City. One of the policeman, who was working as a bodyguard that day, approached me. He wanted a photograph with him, his partners, and Isaac Hayes. They all posed and I took some shots. The policeman gave me his card. After I got the prints to *The Bronx Times*, I mailed the policeman copies as a Christmas present. He sent me a Christmas card back, thanking me for the pictures.

Good Cop, Bad Cop

Carol West
April 26, 2000

One Sunday night during an early cold spell, I walked from 14th Street to Midtown, because I had no token. I had stopped to rest, read, and warm up at Barnes and Noble's on 22nd Street before going on.

I hit my stride on the last leg of my trek and approached the old post office building at 9th Avenue and 30th Street. A police vehicle had stopped and was shining its headlights on people lying under blankets on the large steam grates.

Without getting out of his car the officer called out over his loudspeaker: "You have to move." Bundles of humanity slowly got up hanging on to blankets for warmth. "You can't stay here, you have to go!" Go where? I wondered. No offer of a shelter, nowhere to go.

It was like looking at a blinded deer frozen in the headlights. The homeless just stood there. I walked on wondering if the people would be arrested or if they would walk away, and when the police left would they run back to reclaim their spaces on the warm grates and find any belongings left behind? I wondered if anyone made it to a shelter and was turned away.

I must say the policeman didn't sound like he liked what he was doing, and there was no enthusiasm in his voice. He didn't get out of his warm car on that bitterly cold night. The next day I looked in the papers, but there was no police report of anyone frozen to death.

Cops

Ronnie Eisen
March 19, 1999

It would have to be in
East New York
It seems the police are
A law unto themselves
Spending their days harassing
Harmless girls
Who sit on boxes
All day long
Because there is nothing to
Do in the shelter at all.

"Don't go in the vacant lot"
Screamed the cop.
"You do that again
And I'll lock you up!"
Who knew an abandoned lot
Was now a forbidden
Zone to the homeless
Girls who hang around?

"Don't touch these dogs,"
Yelled the policemen.
I didn't even see him.
"Is that your dog, lady?"
I said, "No way, sir.
I live in a shelter.
I never knew her."

"Why is she pregnant?"
I looked around
And cursed myself.

It Really Pisses Me Off...

Nelson Blackman
April 15, 1998

1. When I don't get enough sleep. When I was homeless for two years I would sleep on the subway. But I'd get woken up by the police officers every twenty minutes.
2. People who make false accusations against someone else.
3. When I see injustice all around me.
4. Child labor, when people make their kids work, like in those old photographs by Louis Hines and Jacob Riis.
5. Police brutality. At the Harlem Jazz Festival, the police were harassing black and Latino teenagers. I was drinking tea and a cop stopped me and asked, "Can I see what's in your bottle?" I showed him that it was just tea. He was hassling me for no reason.

Why Get Involved

Dorothy Jackson
April 21, 2004

The shelter system stinks. They are counterproductive and very dysfunctional. We never get the desperately needed assistance and services
we need to get on our feet and stay on our feet, like increasing benefits for relief recipients and those on Social Security or disability. We
are not treated with respect and kindness from the shelter staffs, not
the majority of them anyway.

It Really Pisses Me Off...

Carol West
April 19, 2000

On Holy Thursday at Holy Apostles Soup Kitchen in Chelsea it's a sunny spring day for everyone to get out and enjoy themselves. At 10:30 a.m., we volunteers begin serving lunch of turkey tetrazzini, two veggies, and fruit cocktail to hungry guests, adding bread and lemonade to fill their trays.

The word is out: Mayor Giuliani is across the street. Is he visiting Chelsea Health Center, no? Is he stopping by to see our efforts to feed one thousand hungry homeless New Yorkers every weekday? Well, no, he's going to dedicate a handball court nearby. Some luncheon guests express a desire to eat their lunch *al fresco* near the mayor and off go a group with their trays.

I wonder myself if the mayor might be a bit peckish and offer to take him a tray on the spot. We have a good chef, Chris O'Neill, and the meal is free. "No, dish up," I'm quietly reminded. "Our guests are more important."

The mayor made a quick "speak and run" appearance guarded by a phalanx of security, and by the time the guests arrived the mayor was gone. The police were left behind to keep the guests quietly seated and "in line."

Mayor Giuliani won't be dining with the poor today.

You Can Get Used to Anything

Janice English
April 24, 2002

Sometimes I feel like I'm invisible. No one seems to care what you need, what you say, who you are, or what you want in life. People look at you, take what they need, and go about their business, never caring how you feel or what you're going through. Once in a while you find someone in life who will stop and take a minute to look and see what you are.

I seem to always have this problem. It stems from childhood where my needs weren't met. After a while you don't even know you have needs or desires, or as you get older you forget that at one time, you had dreams or desires because no one validates you. You forget about yourself and you go through life unconscious of who you really are and what you need to be joyful and happy.

I've asked myself, "Janice, is it because you don't ask for what you need?" So I began to tell people my problems and ask for what I needed. And guess what? No help came. There were no solutions, especially from the family I was born into, and my own children and grandchildren as well. They say, "Oh, that's just Mommy or Grandma," not understanding that I'm really hurting inside.

We never know how long we're going to be on this earth, so I believe we should take advantage of the time we have with our loved ones. I pray that one day before I leave this earth, that I'll have someone in my life who will really see and hear me, so I won't be invisible anymore.

You Can Get Used to Anything

Jay Stockman
April 21, 2004

My latest move was to a New York City housing project. This project was near a to-be-finished recreation center boasting a large swimming pool. Since a car wreck did much damage to me forty years ago, this was important. "Just what I need," I said as I moved in. Nearly thirty years later it's still not open. Work has been done though, and it should be ready in at least a month. We'll still see. The harm to my coordination from the lack of regular swimming (until two weeks ago I was able to swim forty minutes per week, now nothing) is bad. Hope becomes large, as I look across the street.

You Can Get Used to Anything

Dorothy Jackson
March 24, 2004

It began November 3, 2002. I fled my apartment because abuse was coming from two different directions—my cousin and my boyfriend. I ended up at a shelter in Harlem on 127th Street and Morningside Drive that allowed you refuge for three weeks.

The Coalition for the Homeless gave me a choice of three armories to go to. I chose Franklin in the Bronx and stayed there for thirty-three days. I was then transferred to Lenox Hill Shelter where I've been for fourteen months. Why so long? It's because I'm very independent, coupled with the fact I'm not a former substance abuser, so my packet for housing is always returned.

Praise Almighty God, on December 4, 2003, I finally received my Section 8 voucher in which I was told I was definitely entitled to consideration. I have applied in every borough but Staten Island.

So I've been looking for housing in Monmouth County, New Jersey, where my oldest son lives on Earle Naval Base and is pursuing a career in computers. You cannot get used to anything in New York.

You Can Get Used to Anything

Joe Negrelli
March 24, 2004

You can get used to anything.

Getting used to being abused is not easy. I felt that I was abused when I was in the hospital for twenty-eight days. Blood every four hours (giving not receiving). Poke! Poke! Poke! Pinch—stab—hurt. No matter how gentle they were I knew they had gotten me. Vials of blood all lined up in a row. Different color tops for who knows what reason. Just all four to six tubes filled to the brim—my precious little red blood. Sometimes I wished I were a Vulcan so it would be green. Give them something to talk about.

No! Some things you can't get used to.

Part 4:

Keeping Hope Alive

The Door Opens

Carol West
April 19, 2000

I've had a lot of doors slammed in my face. In fact, I've helped pull many of them shut. I'm several years into another decade, and I know there's no going back to where I started. Doctors are talking to me about high blood pressure, an aspirin a day, diet, and replacement therapy; but I know I've reached a new door in my life when I hear "at your age."

A "senior moment" becomes a polite phrase for memory lapse. Eyeglasses a defense against smaller print. You see your hair colorist when too much gray shows. You get a senior citizen discount at McDonald's for coffee. A lady got up on a bus to give me her seat. In reading the Help Wanted ads, the phrase "want people with youthful attitudes" jumps off the page. Geritol starts to command your attention, and I peruse "Centrum Silver" vitamins. When asked my age I say "old enough to know better."

I go to the movies for the story and not the star. I don't mind being late anymore. I speak my mind with no apologies. I called my congressman's office and said, "Listen, Sonny, I vote," to the young assistant.

I'm beginning an era in my life's journey where there are no more doors. It's a space of uncharted territory. I take a step forward. I'll draw my own map.

A New Door Opens

Jay Stockman
April 16, 2003

I got notice last week of a meeting I should go to—on the East Side by Bellevue Hospital. This meeting was important to me. It was for a political party made up of disabled people. But when I got there, though it was far from where I live, I heard it was canceled. I thought, "I got here after going through a lot of trouble. I don't want to leave right away." I didn't know what to do.

I decided to explore the neighborhood. After cruising around a supermarket half a block from the supposed meeting, I found a big 99¢ Store. One of the store's workers (at least I thought he was a worker) used a wheelchair. Consequently I found the aisles were uncluttered and large enough for me to pass through with my wheelchair. This store had the same kind of merchandise offered by 99¢ Stores in Chelsea—but even more of it because of its greater size.

I want to go back. The distance is a problem. Maybe I can plan it for before or after the next scheduled meeting in that neighborhood. I should hope the meeting is not canceled—or takes too long a time. But finding that new store was a new delight.

If I Had to Leave Tomorrow

Carol West
April 7, 2004

If I had to leave tomorrow it would be very easy. All that I've held dear has been sold, given away, or shredded. I've learned to live without them, my possessions.

Small coffee table knick-knacks, mementos collected from worldwide trips to Hong Kong, Europe, and across America, have been given away as gifts. Jewelry was traded at a pawnshop to pay rent. Antique furniture from flea markets and from family was sold to live.

As life goes on you need less, want less, expect less, ask less.

Letting go of little parts of me felt like death. But the best is left, memories the way I want to remember, the only possession I'll never lose.

What If I Had to Leave Tomorrow

Joe Negrelli
April 7, 2004

First thing, pack for the trip. Bare essentials. Easier that way, you know.

Find a way to collect and pay the bills. Maybe the next-door neighbor could help.

Make sure I have both medication and medical supplies to travel.

Get to the pick-up location at least a half-hour early so as not to keep people waiting for me.

Never forget to ask the big spirit for assistance in this endeavor. Hey, it never hurts to have an extra pal in your court for anything that may come up.

If I Had to Leave Tomorrow

Tory Connolly Walker
April 7, 2004

If I had to leave tomorrow I'd take warm memories with me of this church, its ministries, this Writers' Workshop, and my new friends from the Soup Kitchen.

Certain faces come to me and the Lord has asked me to pray for people I've met at Holy Apostles as I pray for myself and loved ones. I have many problems, lots of challenges, but who doesn't? The stress of daily living. A place like this gives me sustenance, food to help my sagging finances and therapy for the soul in the Writers' Workshop— a real blessing.

If I had to leave tomorrow I'd pack light. I've always packed way too much for the journey, and old baggage weighs me down. Overcoming alcohol, drugs, and manic-depression has set me free to travel without closets full of old demons that I lugged around for years. If I had to leave tomorrow forever I'd have faith I'd be in my Father's House the next second, for He says: "Absent from the Body. Present with the Lord." I'd sing songs of worship with the saints, warmed by God's fulsome presence as He reveals his many mysteries. I'd be grateful that the time trap of Earth, the mental suffering, stress, and material strife are gone, while we live forever in the Joy of the Lord.

Since I haven't left yet and I'm still here on Earth, I'd like to share a song I wrote about pearls I found. I can't wear them. They belong to my Father and He wears them in His Crown.

Pearls in a Soup Kitchen
Diamonds are a girl's best friend
(so they say)

And Pearls are a rare, rare find
Gold just "don't" manifest every day
(so they say)
But there is treasure beyond measure
Of another kind.

There are Pearls in a soup kitchen
Oh, who knew you could find?
Friends and Diamonds in a Soup Kitchen
Well it kind of blows your mind.

'Cause God's in this Soup Kitchen
Writing new names in the Book of Life
Serving food through servants, yes
But the Lord also
Stands in line.

Yet He's King and Majesty
Healer and Provider
The Bread of Life,
O Jehovah Jireh

Redeemer, Savior
And The Rose of Sharon
He's our Father
Who never stops caring.
Diamonds are a girl's best friend
(so they say)
And a Pearl is a rare, rare find
Jewels don't manifest every day
(so they say)

Yet there is treasure beyond measure
Of another kind.
For the Pearls in this Soup Kitchen
Will be Diamonds in His crown
Believing children in His
Kingdom yes
Who were lost,
But now are found
We were lost but
Now are found
Diamonds, Pearls and Emeralds
In His crown

The Rest of the Story

Carol West
April 18, 2001

My ex-husband sent me a card for spring from his home in England. The spidery writing from my past sent a chill down my spine. The ghostly missive from my youth beckoned me to take sides in an ongoing in-law war. My best friend said, "You should have shot him ten years ago, and you'd have no worries."

I wasn't going to be haunted by old problems till my niece Jill wrote with the other side of the story. A three-page Gothic saga ensued of illness, breakdowns, accusations, bitter phone calls, and hospitalizations.

My ex, "Reggie," and his other sister, "Queenie," were driving my niece and her mother, "Maude," crazy. It was one of those situations where I didn't ask, and was sorry to find out more than I wanted to know.

The chains of memories haunt us. I'm writing back and telling everyone to play nice, not to rattle my bones, and leave me out of it. In the future, I'm going back to letting sleeping ghosts lie.

The Rest of the Story

Joe Negrelli
March 3, 2004

Reaching my fifth year as a survivor of a major heart attack this is now a turning point in my life. The fifth year means that you have lived or will tolerate all types of abuse as the result of a heart attack and the subsequent bypass surgery. Bleeding, aches and pains of all types, bandages, pills, tests, and whatnot are boring and annoying.

At this point one is aware of all sorts of things, least of all financial devastation and the additional problems that are accompanied from that aspect alone. I now have been assured that I will fulfill the twenty- to twenty-five-year life span after the doctors' brutality and abuse.

May all be good with those here, and thanks to my friends at Holy Apostles Soup Kitchen, whose constant support never ceases to amaze me.

The Long Winter

Walter L. Schubert
April 9, 2003

Goethe said that for a man's life to be successful it must be lived as an allegory. A beat poet of the '50s compared life to coasting down a hill, mindless of the fact that, eventually, the free ride will come to an end.

I do not see my life this way. Rather, looking back and looking ahead, I see life as a long winter journey. Every so often one sees a blade of dried grass or a nesting place under a shelter. For the most part one ought not to expect that life will be rosy. Doing so will breed complacency and vulnerability.

There are paths one might pursue to make the pain more tolerable. The stories of Greek antiquity have had much to say about this, but too I find that today's "stories" are ascetic and unable to enjoy themselves during periods when we are blessed with plenty.

Yes, prayer has been practiced throughout the ages as a way to deal with hardship. But in a predominantly secular world, resorting to prayer can be misunderstood as an escape from what is popularly regarded as "reality."

Some see hope and resignation as the only two ways to deal with difficulties. There is doubt as to what we ought to love, and whether resignation would be appropriate were we to learn that we had hoped for the wrong thing.

At the close of *Die Winterreise*, Franz Schubert's lieder cycle about a long winter's journey, the singer stumbles into the final passage of the cycle. What was it that sustained him for this trip? The answer: "Think not on my words, for words can always be used to tell a lie. Think instead about my music, for with music one can only say what is there." It was only with my music that I told the truth.

The Best Winter Day

Ronnie Eisen
March 12, 2001

It was a cold snowy day in February. I was not working at the time. I read in the newspaper that the Metropolitan Museum of Art in Manhattan was having a free lecture on Polynesian art. I have always had a fascination for primitive art because I am an artist myself. I enjoy the connection with spirituality and nature that many primitive tribes display in their artwork. It fascinates me that these people with no formal education or tools were able to create such beautiful objects. So I hopped on a subway to attend the early morning lecture at the Met.

It turned out to be a lovely tour and lecture in the Oceania Room at the museum. Our tour guide kept us interested with anecdotes about the different tribes and their works of art. One of the most horrible stories he told us was about the disappearance of Michael Rockefeller while on an expedition to an island to collect Polynesian art. To this day, no one is certain of what happened to him. He may have died in an accident, or even in a flood, but no one has ever seen him again.

The best part of the day was when I left the museum. The snow had stopped, and Central Park was covered in a blanket of white. Hundreds of birds were singing. I went into the park and slid down one of the hills. While I was playing this silly game, I noticed a man watching me. I stared back at him because he seemed familiar. It was then that I realized he was the actor, Keanu Reeves. I was so shocked I didn't even know how to say hello. Of all my winter days in New York—it was my most interesting of all.

At the Beach

Janice English
April 4, 2001

I love going to the beach. Every year since I can remember my children, and now my grandchildren, always go to the beach when it gets warm. I consider it our family ritual. Usually we go to Coney Island because of the rides and because there is no time limit on how long you can stay.

The other beaches we go to are Jones Beach or Orchard Beach in the Bronx. They usually make you leave the beach around seven or eight in the evening. When we go to Coney Island, we get home around four or five in the morning, because we love the beach so.

Sometimes when I need a boost, I go out to the beach by myself. It doesn't matter what the weather is, I just hop on the train and there I go out there to play, to talk to the Goddess of the Water—Yemaya. I ask for guidance. At these times the beach makes me feel peaceful and serene.

On one of these solitary visits, I took the train to Coney Island. The sun was not shining that day, but I needed to go anyway. When I reached the boardwalk it was extremely foggy, so foggy that you couldn't see the beach. At first I just stood on the boardwalk and then I decided, what the hell.

I began walking towards the water. I never walked through a fog before. It was such an eerie feeling. I felt like I was in a scene from a movie. I wondered if this was what heaven felt like.

I made it to the water and sat on the rocks. In the silence I meditated, and it was one of the most beautiful experiences. I felt as if I was the only person on Earth, and there was no way anyone could find me in the fog.

At the Beach

Carol West
April 4, 2001

I entered the world as a honey-blond, blue-eyed baby, with milky white skin.

Before my fourth birthday, the old woman who babysat me left me out in the sun all day, and I had a bad sunburn that did not abate for three days. I cried continuously from the pain. After that, my relationship with this heavenly body that is the giver of life has been tenuous at best.

I dated and married a man who loved and worshiped the sun. He could stand on the sand by the water for five minutes and get a kiss of bronze in return. After one day he could have been a model for a swimsuit ad.

The first summer I tried to tan I went easy. I used the most expensive sun lotions, but I got sun poisoning, sunburn, and a bit of sunstroke. That was just the first day. I was told "it will get better." Week after week it never did. I peeled and looked like a lobster.

When I started working for the airlines, I found it was easier to fly to uncrowded St. Thomas rather than drive three hours each way to the nearest beach. I sat in the shade of the bar and drank daiquiris, and shouted, "Enjoying yourself, honey?" as my Beach Babe happily played in the water and worked on his golden tan. I saw his hair turn blonde. He was a god. It was a religious experience watching him.

We moved to Florida for a year. My skin flaked, I got freckles, and developed "brown spots" even though I stayed inside or covered up in the shade. My husband lived in the sun, recharging his batteries. I moved back to New York, and had to go to a dermatologist. He said, "You can't go out into the sun anymore. Your skin is damaged from sunbathing twenty years ago, and it could be precancerous."

Twenty years of a day at the beach.

At the Beach

Thyatira English
April 4, 2001

When I was thirteen years old, I had a friend named Kisha, who lived across the street from us. She would come over from time to time to spend the night. So one time in the summer, when it was really hot, my mother said, "Let's go to the beach."

Kisha had a radio, so my mother asked her to bring the radio. So she did. We got our stuff ready. We lived in the Bronx at that time, and my mother liked to go to Coney Island, which is a two-hour train ride.

We were riding on the train and my mother said, "Play some music on the radio." But you could only play CDs or tapes, and Kisha had only brought one tape, by the group *All 4 One*—that song "I Swear." It was bad.

We thought my mother had brought tapes, but she hadn't brought anything. So for the whole way to Coney Island we listened to that one tape. When we finally got outside, we tuned off the tape and put on the radio so we could listen to some other music.

When I see Kisha, we talk about the time we went to the beach with one tape. Sometimes when I hear the song, I laugh.

The Beach

Donald Mackey
March 27, 1996

About eight years ago, I had my four smallest children at the beach. After we had enjoyed playing and eating, after I had given them swimming lessons, I was all packed and ready to take them home. As I turned to make sure that we were together, I looked and saw them all standing near the ocean shore. They were holding hands as they stood in perfect stair fashion. Awesomely silent. I wish I had a camera. There is just something about that sight that I don't believe I shall ever forget.

That summer moment that I love so much was abruptly interrupted when another child, who was playing with a large stick, ran by me and accidentally rapped me on the knuckles. It hurt badly. At the moment of impact of that stick on my hand. I realized how happy I had been for just a few seconds.

The Morning Glory

Leucio Parella
April 23, 1998

The scent of morning glories is delightful.
The morning glory is a peaceful flower.
Yes, a tingle goes up my spine in this garden of delight.
Would you walk on the green grass with bare feet?
Would you see a waterfall in this garden of my creation?
Would you sit with me under the peaceful trees?
Would you let me read you a poem?
It elevates me in the morning sun.
Would you join me with a morning glory tea
In my special garden where I go when I'm lonely?

September Eleven

Jay Stockman
May 8, 2002

September 11 was a Primary Day in New York. As a poor person with a disability, I jump at each chance I get to work at the polls. The payment is paid to a voter number. So it is anonymous; there's no official record. So folks who are not really eligible can work that day. I went to my polls (where I also vote) at 5:30 a.m. Things went well until a little past 9. Then people who worked there got a TV set up in the auditorium. We had a live TV view of what was going on at the World Trade Center. The polls were closed by 11. Going outside, I saw a huge cloud where I thought Canal Street was. Despite the ongoing tragedy downtown, the kitchen here was open and we served food to the hungry that day.

September 11, 2001

Carol West
May 8, 2002

Some day I'll write of seeing thousands of bodies going up in pillars of white smoke, how the smell of death went on for weeks.

I want to write a former sister-in-law in England and say, "For a moment, I had a glimmer of what you lived through in the London Blitz." But I couldn't write that.

I sent my former husband a postcard of the Twin Towers and said, "Where you worked and the business life you once knew is no more." He wrote back, "I'm just glad you're alive."

Nine-eleven is like the day Kennedy was shot. You remember where you were, but you put the pain away.

September 11

Ted Sikorski
May 8, 2002

I was sitting outside, reading *The New York Times* that Tuesday morning. Between reading a few sentences, I glanced up from the newspaper and watched people hurry by. There seemed to be nothing special to see that morning. The weather was exquisite. The sky was deep blue, the air clean and fresh. The day before, I had had an important meeting at the World Trade Center complex. Because it had gone well I now had a sense of peace and calm.

Cars, taxis, buses, and trucks passed by me on the busy thoroughfare, while I sat and read the newspaper. I had grown accustomed to the noise. People continued to pass by while I continued to read the paper. Many were going to work. Others walked their children to school. A jogger ran by.

All of a sudden, I heard a loud roar coming from above, like thunder. The noise grew louder by the second. It was deafening, like the sound of jet engines. Something here was amiss. The only other time I had heard a similar sound in the city was during Fleet Week, when the military was in town. The sound was very loud, a deafening roar.

I looked up, and caught a glimpse of a jumbo jet flying overhead. It was flying unusually low, just above the tops of the buildings. I clearly saw the jet, its cabin windows, and its two large engines giving off the deafening sound. The jet appeared to be flying the length of Manhattan, due south. The jet was swaying back and forth, as if it were experiencing trouble. It was flying erratically. A woman who was walking by was having difficulty holding back tears. "Someone with personal problems," I thought. Then another woman followed, also in tears. I put aside my newspaper and began to watch intently. Several people were crying openly. Most unusual. The jet had flown over my head a few minutes before, but I dismissed any notion of a connection between the plane and tears.

Finally out of curiosity I stood up and approached one of the women. I asked politely whether something had just happened. I suspected a vehicular accident. I was wrong. The accident was much more severe. "A plane smashed into the north tower of the World Trade Center," she said. I took several steps into the street, turned my head and saw the large gaping hole in the building. I flashed back to the jumbo jet that had just flown by . . . .

September 11

Joe Negrelli
March 10, 2004

I knew a young man named Patrick Brown who was a captain in the FDNY Engine Company 3. Pat and I knew each other for more than ten years. We went for walks and talks and to the beach. He was a character, a strong virile male whose life was quite different than mine—Irish Catholic ex-Marine, who from the time he was a little boy always wanted to be a fireman.

I remember once I asked him, "If you hadn't become a fireman, what would you be?" He looked at me and said, "Now, Joe, I never thought of ever becoming anything else."

He liked black coffee and hamburgers medium rare. He loved women (all types) and was always happy when they responded to his greetings. Pat was a good-natured character, but a character nonetheless.

He died somewhere in the World Trade Center. Probably one of the upper floors. They found his body on October 19, 2001, but he wasn't buried until November 7, 2001. His funeral was at St. Patrick's Cathedral near Rockefeller Center. So funny for a guy who didn't attend services there. Six blocks were blocked off for his special day. He would have been proud. He did like attention but never grandstanded.

I Made It Myself

Joe Negrelli
March 3, 2004

Since I am very unimaginative I don't make much myself. However, I do some cooking, mostly cleaning up of items thrown about.

I don't know how to describe my creations but okay and good are words that make me feel better about just my little collection of dishes.

So yes, I made it myself.

I Made That

Jeff Rubin
March 10, 2004

My first year in Oliver Wendell Holmes Junior High School, I was thirteen. We were assigned Shop, which everyone had to take. I had the misfortune to be assigned to Mr. Bielski's ceramics class. Now Mr. Bielski was notorious. Everybody hated him. So there I was, stuck in Mr. Bielski's class. To break up the boredom of making ashtrays and vases, a kid named Aldo Pastorelli would take the clay, which was real modeling clay and had to be fired in a kiln and then glazed. Well, anyway Aldo would take the clay and squat like he was taking a dump, which cracked the whole class up. Of course, when Bielski wasn't looking.

Then one day in class Aldo had this bright idea. He knew I could sculpt pretty well and wanted me to sculpt a male organ and put it on the water fountain so not only would the class see but Bielski as well. When the class saw it they all began to laugh hysterically. When Bielski heard the commotion he ran over to the water fountain. He was not so amused. He yelled, "Who did this?" No one in the class would answer. Then Bielski yelled again, "Whoever did this is going to the principal." Then I 'fessed up and said, "I made that," as I thought I was going to the principal's office. He chuckled out loud and said, "Not bad, my boy." Needless to say I got an A.

Volunteering

Jay Stockman
March 24, 2004

Holy Apostles began by feeding between thirty to forty folks gathering in a park across from Holy Apostles. Now it feeds about twelve hundred meals every weekday. I've been with it since 1982, trying different jobs as the kitchen grew. Though people come to the soup kitchen with many social problems, its main job is to feed the hungry. The kitchen tries to also help with other needs—for example, the writing program run by skilled college writing teachers. There's a quarterly, the *Soup Scoop*, we can write for. I like being an active provider in the special program that feeds the hungry. My twice-daily Buddhist chanting gives consistency to my participation here. As I help feed the hungry, I feed myself too.

Recovering

Donald Mackey
May 1, 1996

I am up to my neck in optimism. Wow, I really felt great writing that sentence because last year this time I was in over my head in pessimism. I still had hope, but I just didn't see a breakthrough.

I am now out of the shelter system, and I am living in a private home in Queens. Just the other day I was doing grocery shopping at a St. Albans supermarket. I kept running into the same lady in several aisles, and each time her shopping cart blocked my passage.

The third time this happened, I was about to be annoyed when I suddenly recalled the times when I was tired, homeless, and hungry. I would peer into supermarket windows, watching people going about their normal shopping routines, wishing that my life was that normal again. Noticing that I was displaying impatience, the lady glanced at me and rolled her eyes. I smiled at her, trying to show patience.

Suddenly I appreciated the great changes I made in my life. I am presently completing a book. I am fine-tuning a one-man, one-act play I have written. I am in the process of contacting family members who I have not seen for a while. I am practicing my art as an herbal craftsman. Best of all, since this time last year I completed the course of study at a theological institute. I am now a licensed minister. Today when I leave the Writers' Workshop I am scheduled to visit a sick church member at Brooklyn Hospital. I feel very thankful I can help someone else.

Recovery

Pierce McLoughlin
April 15, 2000

A lot of what I was introduced to as a kid was out of my league. My mother desperately wanted me to be an intellectual (maybe make some contribution to higher education as a Ph.D.). Although my mother was talented as a writer and lecturer, I really did not have her charisma. She lectured on family and religion and the like, but I didn't have her abilities.

As time went by I was pushed from grade level to grade level. Always there was the promise that someday I would be talented and an up-and-coming "professional" at something. It never happened.

In 1967 I decided not to go on—literally. I took advantage of my brother's good graces, staying at his home. Then after fourteen years of drinking and dickering at various jobs, I took a strange leap into the East River.

After being rescued from the East River by the police, I was locked up in a psych ward for ten weeks. The experience gave me time to look at my life and the mess I made of things. My priorities shifted completely. I knew now that priority one had to be sobriety.

Over the last twenty years, I've learned just to be me. Maybe I can still write a few books, but I'm not desperate to do so. Today I have a lot of recovering friends and, most important, peace of mind. I am not much or famous, but I've learned to live in my own skin. One day at a time.

Miracles

Paul Coleman
March 12, 1997

Enough said I'm alive
Twenty years on and off
Many more hope to come
Many more years be done
You tell me what's become
Of the child that was
The winner

I've kept my body clean
I've kept myself in a bubble
Used to be so discreet
Would never get into trouble
I always took the road
Least traveled so now
I pay for that, befuddled

Recovery

Norman Clayton
April 21, 2004

Everything good in my life came from my mother. She taught me patience, charity, tolerance. But with me the road went down and up. I found dead-ends like drugs, alcohol abuse, and gambling. I learned there were bridges over addictions, big, small, short, tall bridges; usually they came in the form of brotherhood. I sought my soul but could not see. I sought my God but he eluded me. I sought my brothers and sisters and finally found all three.

Recovering

Dorothy Jackson
April 14, 2004

I am one of the people who has difficulty finding housing.

I received my Section 8 voucher December 4, 2003, and I decided to transfer this voucher to Monmouth County, New Jersey, where my oldest son lives now. I'm being denied an apartment because of bad credit ratings, and I'm also being denied shelter in this system because I have recently lived in the county. So last Monday and Tuesday night I slept on the Number 1 train. Wednesday morning I ended up on the steps of old friend, and she took me in.

This is not a city or country where anyone should be going through all these changes after being in the shelter system consistently for seventeen months.

On the last Tuesday in January, I was at the meeting at Coalition for the Homeless. Getting involved means surrendering yourself, your entire being to one cause. Getting involved means effective, productive, and positive changes being made for the poor and for those on fixed incomes so that we can get out of these financial ruts. Getting involved means keeping hope alive. Thanks for listening.

Ten Rules for Living

Mitch Wiater
April 25, 2001

1. Have a happy childhood.
2. Be in good health without illness.
3. Get a good education from school and home.
4. Make a lot of friends who are good.
5. Get a good job, work hard, and be enthusiastic about it.
6. Marry somebody valuable, and love each other.
7. Have a lot of children, and teach them how to be good.
8. Be honest and help other people.
9. Take care of yourself and your family.
10. Try to be happy, even when you are not happy.

Ten Rules for Living

Janice English
April 25, 2001

1. Your feelings are important. A lot of times in childhood our parents or teachers do not acknowledge our feelings, so we grow up feeling unworthy and that our feelings don't count. This messes us up because we learn to doubt ourselves and what we are feeling. Usually the first thought is the right thought.

2. We are responsible for ourselves. Nobody wants to hear this, but know that although there is a God/Goddess, we do have control over how we respond to the situation we are in. We can either take the high road or the low road. It's really up to us.

3. Your family comes first. No matter how much money you have, there is no fun spending it without people that you truly love and who truly love you. Care for them and show them that you love them always. Don't hide how you feel. If you're sad, let them know. If you're happy, let them know that too.

4. Keep praying. It's what keeps us connected to God/Goddess, the spirits that watch over us, the angels. I'm amazed at the number of people who don't pray. Even if you feel your prayers aren't being answered the way you want, believe that they are heard.

5. Health is extremely important. Without your health, you have nothing. No matter how much money you have, you still have nothing. Make health a priority in your life and your children's lives as well.

6. We need money to live in this world. It has taken me a long time to get this, but without a substantial income to live on, you leave yourself open to the control of others. I used to be one of those people who said, "Oh, money isn't important to me," but I realize now that it is. I now cringe when I hear other people say that.

If you have these thoughts, see where in your life you don't value yourself. It usually stems from feelings of unworthiness you had as a child.

7. Always honor yourself. Easier said than done. Keep your word to yourself and others, but especially yourself. If you don't keep your word to others, they'll know you lack integrity and won't want to be bothered. If you don't honor yourself, you can't expect anyone else to honor you.

8. Words have power. Always be careful what you say, to the chatter-chatter inside yourself and to others outside yourself. If you do speak negatively, you'll find that the negative will be drawn to you like a magnet. Most of us complain all the time. Begin to catch yourself when you do this. Stop complaining about yourself and others, because we all have issues.

9. Learn to be quiet. Always seek quiet time alone. Most people don't like silence. But in the silence, you can hear the voice of God/Goddess, ancestors, or whatever you believe in. There is strength in being still. Spend some sort of time in silence every day.

10. Love yourself. We have been taught to hate ourselves, big time. But if we don't love ourselves, how can others truly love us? If we don't love ourselves, good things won't come to us. If we truly love ourselves, all the challenges won't necessarily go away, but it will make our life easier. This is something I'm still working on and probably always will be.

Ten Rules for Living

Joe Negrelli
March 31, 2004

1. The first would be the easiest. Wake up every day (could be night or afternoon).
2. Get out of bed.
3. Clean up a little. You feel better when you take a shower or a bath.
4. Eat or drink something good for yourself. Not a bottle of beer.
5. Get dressed like you're going somewhere. No bathrobes, underwear, or the natural look.
6. Take five minutes or more to center yourself. Ask your greater spirit to guide you through this day.
7. Think positive. A good attitude goes a long way.
8. Give thanks to the world for this grace. A) Speak kindly to someone on the street. B) Thank the bus driver or conductor for his assistance in getting you there. C) Smile and many people will smile back—or move away from you.
9. Reinforce your meditation with your greater spirit. Sometimes it helps to check in with this loving inner force.
10. Make sure you have told all your loved ones (including friends) how much they mean to you. You can write a note or make a call.

Ten Rules for Living

Peter Nkruma
March 31, 2004

1. Be Idealistic. Whether it's in the philosophical concept of the Good, or the Judeo-Christian God, or in the nebulous Brahman, idealism transforms our primal nature into something higher.
2. Protect Idealism. Whether it is in a child's love of nature, or in an idea of international law, protect idealism in all its forms with all your strength because it is incredibly rare.
3. Feel Compassion. Direct goodwill out in the world. It is hard to hold onto a petty grudge when you know that the object of your disdain, like you, is living on this planet briefly and then passing away. Compassion for a fellow mortal puts it all into perspective.
4. Pray or Meditate. We must pay attention to our inner needs. This can take the form of a novena, or a yoga asana or a Tibetan Buddhist chant. It will strengthen sanity, bring unity to our complex drives, and help attain a strong "I," while bringing us closer to the ultimate "Other."
5. Create. How else will anyone know that you have been a part of life? Write, play music, paint, sculpt, or draw. Show the world what you are artistically.
6. Be a Maverick. Go where no one else has gone before. Do what no one else has done before you. Call life an adventure and solve it in a way that no one else ever has.
7. Be Curious. For some bizarre reason, we have curbed the idea of learning into the first eighteen years of life, and only then to learn how to do a trade, spend the rest of our lives doing that trade until retirement. Learning should never stop.
8. Don't Be Materialistic. Show me how a man treats another man, and you'll see how he treats himself. Violent emotions and black

thoughts arise from the futile attempt to grab onto the ever-changing world and its seductive charms.

9. Improvise. There are no set formulas to life. Play it by ear, learn, do good in many ways, explore beauty, improvise.

10. Edit. Learn from your mistakes and apologize when an apology is needed. Use results gained from your curiosity to do things better. Improvise better until you can improvise no more.

Nine Rules for Not Living

Carol West
March 12, 1997

I never went skiing. I know that with my grace and balance I would have ended up with two broken legs and broken arms.

I never carried a child to full term and gave birth.

I never went to the Statue of Liberty. Going by on the Staten Island Ferry not the same.

I never had the guts to walk into a snooty store and try on Mr. Armani's clothes.

I never met the president of the United States in person. Even if I did, would it really mean anything and would he shake my hand?

I never went to a Knicks game. Even in the peanut gallery I'd probably try and wave to a player and say hi.

I never went to Montreal, Canada. At twenty, no desire. At thirty-five, because my ex-husband went. Now at forty, something interesting, an abusive French experience in North America.

I never had the follow-through to write a producer, a director, a writer, and say I have an idea to make your show, your column, your work better. If you could just tell me if you like it and where I can sell it.

I never have been brave.

Religion

Nelson Blackman
March 8, 2000

Is there anyone who understands life?
What is the purpose of our existence?
Does anyone know if there is a God or not?
If he does exist, why did he create sadness?
Parents and priests put ideas and misconceptions
In our minds, principles both good and bad.
But church is not a structure or a building
Made by man. Religion is in your heart.

Religion

Carol West
April 24, 2002

My grandmother always told me, "A thank-you and a smile go a long way," almost every day. It usually works when you are younger and prettier. Nowadays, in the "rude" generation, people seem surprised if you thank them for help, a favor, money, or gifts.

People who expect to get a thank-you usually don't.

"Thank you" is a magic word people remember. Jesus must have expected a thank-you when he cured ten lepers, but only one returned in gratitude. "Didn't I cure ten?" he asked.

I have a gratitude list of five items I put in a journal every day. It reminds me of small victories, and the little and big kindnesses of life.

Mornings when I awake, I always say, "Thank you, God, I have another day."

Religion

Jay Stockman
March 9, 1995

I live in the Elliot-Chelsea Houses—a housing project on West 25th–27th Streets between 9th and 10th Avenues. I first came there while desperately looking for a place to live that I could afford on a small income. Elliott-Chelsea is a good place for me. There are four supermarkets within two to three blocks. There's buses and subways available. I also need a good shoe repair place close by, and that's there too. Plus the rent is affordable. Nearby is the Church of the Holy Apostles. Most of my neighbors go to St. Columba, a Roman Catholic church on the next block. Yet Holy Apostles is the source of a job for me. It also hosts the soup kitchen with good meals and this writing class.

The church's religion is Episcopalian. I have been an Soka Gakkai International Buddhist for more than ten years. This form of Buddhism features a personal altar, daily chanting, and limited structure of religious personnel. A close friend introduced me to it. My daily practice is done alone. I get a weekly newspaper and a monthly magazine, which give some form to my practice. Regular meetings are held weekly at members' houses. Whenever you want to go, there's a place for chanting and shopping at the bookstore. Or you can take part in activities held at the Culture Center on Union Square East. Practice is a personal affair.

Religion

Joe Negrelli
April 2, 2003

As a relatively new volunteer to the Holy Apostles Soup Kitchen I would like to thank all volunteers who've made my time here enjoyable.

I originally came as a guest to the Kitchen. I noticed those volunteers who took their position seriously and those who possibly took less care in their position. Yes the guests do indeed notice such things. While waiting in line you do have a lot of free time. Depending on the weather conditions the line moves slowly at different points.

When I was able to consider volunteering I first went back to my doctor to ask if it posed any possible health risk. After getting the all-clear I approached Clyde (known to everyone on line) and asked if he needed additional help. I was in luck that he had an opening that day.

Like most others my first position was spoons, and nobody ran out or ate without a spoon that day. Not because of my great effort but of the efforts of all volunteers doing their assignments. Like a finely tuned machine, many parts working together.

The volunteers have misconceptions about the guests. Some believe that all guests are drug- or alcohol-addicted. Others feel that many guests have health concerns of their own making (AIDS, HIV, or hepatitis C). As if getting fired, laid off, or terminated for any of a thousand reasons is your own fault. Disease is not of our own making.

"All guests are welcome here" is the church rule. People who show up here between 10:30 a.m. and 12:25 p.m. will be fed regardless. Those who show up drunk or high are sometimes asked to eat outside. The rules are minimal. As most know we also have the trailers outside for additional types of referrals. Wednesday is "Writers' Workshop."

Thursday is "Legal Clinic" and "Chiropractics." In the winter we get hats, coats, and scarves from Jackie, and on holidays, we often get ice cream and toiletries as an extra special treat.

It's fun being a guest, but it's also nice to volunteer and give back service to both the other volunteers and the others in the line, who know that we can be both guest and volunteer.

Because of Holy Apostles I was able to change my life. Because of my fellow guests I was given encouragement to be an advocate for myself.

Religion

Muhammad Siagha
March 17, 2004

True love is a woman laying down becoming a mother, creating a being which in my eyes is an angel, while the man stands guard and becomes a father under the sun, moon, and stars. It's not our fault we don't understand. We were never told the whole truth. No one ever showed or taught us how to see past the ceiling or the roof.

If I were a millionaire instead of homeless, I would build a hospital with a clear roof, so that every woman becoming a mother, creating a being which in my eyes is an angel, would have a window to see the sky. Then it would be an actual fact that everyone was born under the sun, moon, and shining stars.

Religion

Clarence A. Clarke
May 1, 1996

Since 1964 nearly all my waking hours have been occupied with study of Christian metaphysics. This means that whatever I engage in by ways of employment, whether self-employment or otherwise, what I've learned in Christian Science is applied with as much sincerity as I can muster.

It is not surprising that I have concluded that being here has not come about by accident, or human will, or human ambition, but because of divine providence and the plan of God. There are a number of signs that have led me to think this.

Foremost of these is the fact that my status in the United States of America has not been formalized sufficiently by citizenship. Yet it is a matter of no great concern to me or anybody else. Neither the U.S. government nor any official agency raises any question. I am even given a unique number that I use for official identification.

However, I am aware that it is necessary to take the further steps to make my citizenship status legal, especially remembering what my mission is: "Heal the sick, cleanse the lepers, cast out demons, raise the dead, preach the Gospel to the poor."

Writing

John Cabello
April 7, 2004

It was nice
Today, writing on
Two topics.

To write poetry
Sometimes
Is so easy.

Other times
It becomes
So slow

So slow until the time
To finish writing
Is announced.

Like just
A sentence
Really rough.

When such
Deep feelings
Are still ahead.

To be written on
A sheet of
Paper really

Roughly not
Thrown but
As kindly kissing

Sharing words
It really felt good
To write today

A Writing Fable

Carol West
December 5, 1997

In the spring of 1963, I was a junior in high school going nowhere and trying to fit in somewhere. The worst thing anyone could ask me was, "What do you want to be when you grow up?" I didn't know.

It was assumed in a southern "Cinderella" fantasy, by my hopeful family, that SOMEDAY I could find some little job, meet the "right guy," date, get married, and be a "homemaker." I wanted something, but this scenario was not my agenda.

Spring was wonderful that year; you could smell the new earth and a promise of renewal in the air. You felt you could do anything, accomplish any dream. The buds on the trees waited to burst out. It was getting warm, and everyone welcomed the season.

I had a wonderful English teacher that year, Mrs. Clancey. She was so short she just reached five feet in spike heels, but she was a power to be dealt with. She taught us from *Adventures in English Literature*, Chaucer, Shakespeare, Dryden, Tennyson. We chanted of "The Ancient Mariner," "Water, water everywhere," and we read Dickens in depth. She was someone you could talk to, and a mentor you listened to.

When she said write, we wrote. I blossomed in grammar, composition, and vocabulary. I loved going to her class. I felt productive writing. It was an outlet for the creativity of my fantasies and the non-normality of my life.

I became pleased with what I was writing, and after months I took a chance on asking what she thought of my efforts. I had written what I felt was a short, sharp, and funny composition that had been read before a group of "cool" people who thought it amusing and laughed.

On a fine day with gentle sunshine, I saw an opportunity to ask her during study period in the school cafeteria. It was a quiet time when homework could be done. I went up to her as she walked the aisles between tables, and I asked, "What do you think of my writing?" She looked at me, someone who never appeared interested, who had never really made an effort. She thought for long moment, watching me wait for her answer. She finally replied, "I have other students who write much better than you do." She smiled at me, and when I didn't say anything she moved on.

In that one moment my world stopped. I felt the pain of just not being good enough, of failure and disappointment. To this day, whenever I think of that moment, I see the sunny cafeteria full of unfilled promise, full of cool, smart kids I didn't jive with.... I let my writing hopes die. I never bothered to write again. Until three decades later, when I saw a flyer for a writing workshop at Holy Apostles.

Part 5:

Photographs of Contributors

by Nelson Blackman

The Holy Apostles Soup Kitchen

Bob Blaisdell, Mitch Wiater, and Ian Frazier

2002 Workshop with Pierce McLoughlin kneeling in front

Nelson Blackman

Clarence Clarke

2001 Workshop

2004 Workshop

Janice English

Leucio Parella

Tory Connolly Walker

Ted Sikorski

Jay Stockman

Liz Maxwell and Carol West

Donald Mackey

Joe Negrilla

Thyatira English

Jeff Rubin

John Cabello

Norman Clayton